TOM STUART-SMITH
DRAWN FROM THE LAND

TOM STUART-SMITH
DRAWN FROM THE LAND

Tim Richardson

Foreword by Piet Oudolf
With essays by Tom Stuart-Smith

Frontispiece: Hatch House

Page 15: The Barn
Page 65: Encombe
Page 129: Wycliffe Hall
Page 193: Mount St John
Page 249: Moor Hatches

First published in the United Kingdom in 2021 by
Thames & Hudson Ltd, 6–24 Britannia Street, London WC1X 9JD

This compact edition published in 2026

Tom Stuart-Smith: Drawn from the Land © 2021 and 2026
Thames & Hudson Ltd, London

Text © 2021 Tim Richardson, unless otherwise stated

Essay: 'Close Encounters and the View from Above' © 2021 Tom Stuart-Smith

Essay: 'Attachment, Separation and Loss: A Garden Narrative' © 2021 Tom Stuart-Smith, first published in the *Garden Museum Journal,* Issue No. 25, Summer 2011.

Foreword © 2021 Piet Oudolf

Designed by Linda Lundin

All Rights Reserved. No part of this publication may be reproduced or transmitted in any form or by any means, electronic or mechanical, including photocopy, recording or any other information storage and retrieval system, without prior permission in writing from the publisher.

EU Authorized Representative: Interart S.A.R.L.
19 rue Charles Auray, 93500 Pantin, Paris, France
productsafety@thameshudson.co.uk
interart.fr

A CIP catalogue record for this book is available from the British Library

ISBN 978-0-500-03088-2
01

Printed in China by RR Donnelley

Be the first to know about our new releases, exclusive content and author events by visiting
thamesandhudson.com
thamesandhudsonusa.com
thamesandhudson.com.au

CONTENTS

Foreword — Piet Oudolf		6
Introduction — Tim Richardson		8
THE NURTURED SPACE	Broughton Grange	16
	Snowdenham House	26
	House in Kottayam	34
	The Barn	46
PLANTING — Tim Richardson		57
ARCADIA	Charleville	66
	Encombe	76
	Culham Court	88
	Vergelegen	100
	Cogshall Grange	110
CLOSE ENCOUNTERS AND THE VIEW FROM ABOVE — Tom Stuart-Smith		121
TRADITION	Windsor Castle	130
	Wycliffe Hall	140
	Madresfield Court	152
	Yotes Court	162
	Fort Belvedere	174
DESIGN PHILOSOPHY — Tim Richardson		185
SCALE	Trentham	194
	Oakhill	204
	RHS Wisley	212
	Le Jardin Secret	222
	Mount St John	232
ATTACHMENT, SEPARATION AND LOSS: A GARDEN NARRATIVE — Tom Stuart-Smith		241
ARTS & CRAFTS	A Garden in the Surrey Hills	250
	Whitehall Farm	262
	Moor Hatches	272
	Hatch House	282
THE UNGARDENED GARDEN	La Granja Alnardo	292
Career timeline		302
Acknowledgments		318
Image credits		319
Index		320

FOREWORD

Piet Oudolf

Tom and I first met in 2000 when we worked on a Chelsea Flower Show garden together. We became friends through our interest in plants, of course – but it's not only about the plants. It's about making gardens and also how you look at gardens. Tom is a great plantsman, but he is also a great garden maker and designer.

The first time we really got together was at Trentham, when Tom asked me to work with him. That's how we became close friends, through years of talking about possibilities and making plans together. Tom never told me what he thought I should do. He left me to do the master-planning for the area he handed over to me. A lot of people try to take over other people's ideas, but neither Tom nor me are like that. That's why it worked well.

Initially I was amazed by Tom's knowledge of plants. Not many people have that any more. They know some plants and trees, and can recognize how to use them so they look natural. But Tom knows how to play with plants in different ways. From him I learnt that every day you can discover more about plants or look at them in different ways. I was reminded how important it is to really know plants. And I noticed that he knew more than me.

What is clever about Tom's work is that he knows how to hybridize in design. He has grown up in England with its gardens – and in some way his work is still identifiably English. He has moved towards more natural plantings, but you can still see something of the English style in his gardens. It's not that it is traditional, but the formality is still in there. I appreciate that: you should not lose all of what you have grown up with.

In the past, English gardening was more about decoration than design. But if you don't have the design skills, you can only decorate gardens. Tom moved away from that. With his gardens, you can come back in ten years and they might have changed but they will still look good. Often they will look even better.

Tom has always stayed true to his own style. He has never lost his core, his heart – and that is important. You can always recognize his style. He is very open and generous and accepts other input and influences, but he always sticks to who he is. That's the most important thing in a man's life, as well as in a profession like this.

For me, there are only a few good designers working today, and he is one of them. If I needed to trust someone to design my own garden, I would call Tom.

Opposite
The upper terrace at Broughton Grange, this was Tom Stuart-Smith's first major commission, in 2000.

INTRODUCTION
Tim Richardson

The work represented by the 24 projects featured in this book reflects a fundamentally questing imagination, and a related ability to refine and evolve a design methodology to the point of periodic re-invention. Together with the timeline of completed and current projects found at the end of the book, these case studies chronicle the development of Tom Stuart-Smith's career to date.

The story begins with Broughton Grange (2000), a celebrated commission which truly established Stuart-Smith's reputation as a contemporary designer of note, and continues through a number of other spectacular private projects, many of them focused on walled gardens. There are also public and private designs undertaken in a variety of challenging historical settings, as well as a series of experiments in naturalistic planting – in the meadow at the designer's own home, The Barn, at Vergelegen, in Massachusetts, and most recently at La Granja Alnardo in Spain.

In fact, the story really begins in the Hertfordshire countryside in the hamlet of Serge Hill, 40 kilometres (25 miles) northwest of London, where Tom was born and brought up. His childhood home is a substantial Queen Anne house (c. 1710) with Regency additions, at the centre of a 100-hectare (250-acre) estate with walled garden, woodlands, herbaceous borders and a small park descending sharply into a valley bottom with uninterrupted views south. The idea of 'home' has been unusually important to this designer: Tom still lives, with his family, just a few hundred metres away from the 'big house', in a converted barn sited across the lane. Other family members live very close by.

The woods and gardens of Serge Hill House formed the wellspring of Tom's understanding of landscape. In his youth he would assist his father, a barrister, in an activity they called 'wooding'. 'Every single morning of the school holidays we would go off and plant trees or do some woodland thinning,' he recalls. 'We did that three years in a row and got a huge amount done. All these trees we see in the park today, I planted in my late teens and twenties – it's when I got that bug.' Tom's parents also ran a small market-garden business from the walled garden, and during the school holidays Tom and his siblings would work there for an hour a day.

Opposite
The yew terrace at Broughton Grange, one of Tom's early experiments with evergreen sculptural forms, as a counterpoint to herbaceous plantings elsewhere.

'Self-sufficient' and 'nucleated' is how Tom describes family life at Serge Hill with his parents and five brothers and sisters. There was a strong focus on music. 'This family was our entire world,' he says. 'We used to put on our own plays, and every summer there was a week when around twenty people would come and play music. We'd have chamber music and even a little chamber orchestra.' (The impulse towards music-making remains strong among the Stuart-Smiths; private recitals and concerts are convened regularly at The Barn.)

'I think it's quite easy to get buried in a large family, so I felt very strongly that I had to find my own niche,' Tom reflects. 'One of my brothers had already started to get into the trees, but like a great fat cuckoo in the nest, I sort of got in there and took over.' Then at the age of eight, Tom was sent to boarding school, joining an older brother as a chorister in St George's Chapel at Windsor Castle. 'In many ways it was an unusual place,' he says, 'in that between the ages of eight and thirteen, I spent more time singing than in a classroom. We had to learn two instruments. Our sports pitches were in the Home Park, just below the Castle. But it had this romance about it. There is something about being in the chapel, with all the dark wooden carving. It is one of the most intimate ecclesiastical spaces in the world – like being in a beautiful panelled study. Only it's the study of God.'

This early experience of a rigorously professionalized life arguably stood Tom in good stead. As he remarks: 'The biggest thing of all, if you are a chorister, is that by the age of ten you are doing something which is, by any standards, of high quality. There aren't many fields where that is true.'

Public school – Radley College in Oxfordshire – did not prove to be as happy an experience. Tom was following his older brothers (and his father) at the school and says he did not cope well with suddenly being a small fish in a big pond. 'In many ways, it was a huge come-down. Radley did have the capacity for letting creative people survive – but generally it was very sporty and I was always lurking on the fringes of the cricket team. It was all very matey and macho and I couldn't really deal with it. I've never been able to cope with full-on masculine competitiveness.'

'I think that as a fifteen- and sixteen-year-old, I was really not in a good place,' he continues. 'I was trying to be one of the lads – lots of drinking and smoking.' Tom says that everything changed when, to his amazement, one of his teachers encouraged him to 'try for Oxbridge', and ultimately he was offered a scholarship to study natural sciences at Corpus Christi College, Cambridge.

Tom took a year out before university, first studying art history in Venice and then working on sheep stations and building sites in Australia. 'I worked like a dog and had quite a punishing time,' he recalls. 'It was quite bestial, working with animals and some rough people. Yet in a brutal way I loved it. It went to the heart of these two powerful forces in my life – the idea of being an artist or an animal, the "monk or beast" dichotomy [from E.M. Forster's *Howard's End*]. In a way, gardening on the one hand, and being a designer on the other, has been this wonderful way of bringing together these two elements which outwardly seem irreconcilable.'

It was at Cambridge that Tom realized that his professional path would not lead him deeper into science. 'In my first year I came to understand what science is about,' he says. 'I went into it with this vague idea that I could be a Renaissance man – when actually it's all about statistics. What I enjoyed most was zoological dissection.' This brief scientific training at least cemented in him habits of close observation of nature, and an empirical approach, which he would deploy later as a designer.

It was early on during his time at Cambridge, at the age of nineteen, that Tom decided he wanted to go into landscape design, largely because of his 'wooding' experiences at Serge Hill. Through a family friend he was introduced to leading landscape architect Geoffrey Jellicoe, joining him on a walk round the garden at St Paul's Walden Bury, where Jellicoe advised, and later going for tea at his Highgate flat. 'There was me thinking I was going to find out about planting herbaceous borders and things like that,' Tom says, 'but with Jellicoe it wasn't

Opposite
The walled garden at Cogshall Grange, with bronze shelter by architect Jamie Fobert.

Right
A natural garden composed of native plants at Vergelegen, Massachussets, is almost entirely subservient to the view.

like that at all. It was all pretty cosmic. I was a bit bewildered by Jellicoe, but I did think he was pretty extraordinary.' Other early influences were the plantsman, designer and journalist Lanning Roper, and garden designer and historian Penelope Hobhouse, who was a family friend and early mentor.

Tom's mother also had an impact on his gardening life. Together they went to see famous gardens such as Sissinghurst, Hidcote and Westonbirt. She was also a great plants enthusiast – with limits. 'My mother was a supremely creative person, but she put her energy into making books, into cooking and her career as a chief magistrate,' Tom recalls. 'She was not interested in design – so if ever I brought a plant home she would say, "Oh darling, can we put it by the front door?", so that she could have it there, where she could see it and admire it.'

'When I started buying plants at nurseries, when I was about sixteen, I would bring back a couple of specimens and then she would divide them up and propagate them for me,' Tom says. 'She was very good at this, so by the end of summer we would have around thirty plants. There was this wonderful abundance about her whole approach.'

Tom candidly admits that he was fortunate indeed to have had the benefit of contacts such as Penelope Hobhouse so early in his career – though he resists the accusation that he was handed everything on a plate. Coming from a privileged milieu helps, of course, especially in the early stages of a career, but there is a strong argument that if he had been only average as a designer, Tom's career would have faltered, just like anyone else's.

After Cambridge, Tom immediately went up to Manchester University to study for a degree in landscape design. 'The teacher who stood out was Alan Ruff, a proponent of the Dutch heempark movement,' Tom says. 'He was an interesting guy, slightly isolated in the faculty. But those parks so impressed me – this idea that in the middle of the city you had this rough ground where children went to learn how to grow food. I also spent a lot of time in the Rylands Library reading about the history of landscape. I got deeply into the Picturesque, reading Richard Payne Knight and Uvedale Price. And I spent a lot of time drawing.'

On graduating in 1984, Tom was determined to start in the public realm. He worked in Hal Moggridge's practice for two years, which involved large-scale public projects including a nuclear bunker and a reservoir, and then joined Michael Brown, a designer who specialized in social housing. 'I had a lot of respect for Michael,' Tom says. 'He was a strong critic who taught me a lot about design. He was also a very thoughtful, lifelong socialist who couldn't quite cope with some things. I remember when he came to Serge Hill, he just stopped and said, "What is this place, Tom?" I've always been a soft liberal myself and at that stage I didn't want to make gardens for rich private clients. I could never have gone and been Rosemary Verey's gofer. I really only got into garden design through working with Liz Banks.'

Tom joined Elizabeth Banks Associates in 1988 and stayed there for a decade, specializing in historic landscape schemes (a rich seam of work through the 1980s and 1990s). It was here that he met fellow young designer Todd Longstaffe-Gowan, and the two cultivated a fruitful rivalry and friendship over eight years. 'Working for Liz was a great experience,' Tom says. 'She was immensely generous and let us do our own design work. She introduced both Todd and me to a wide range of clients – of whom perhaps the most enduring has been the Royal Horticultural Society.'

The tipping point for Tom's decision to go solo came in 1998, when he was thirty-eight years old ('I was quite old by today's standards', Tom comments), and it was twofold. First, Todd had announced he was leaving the practice, which changed the atmosphere. Second, Tom had been invited to design his debut Chelsea show garden, for Chanel. This was a great success, and as a result

Right
A view of a garden made for the Royal Horticultural Society at Chelsea Flower Show in 2019. Every part of the garden was recycled, most of it to the new garden at RHS Bridgewater.

clients were beginning to approach him directly for work. Up until this moment, Tom had been best known as a landscape designer most at home in historical settings. Now, for the first time on this (very) public stage, he was able to give full rein to his horticultural impulses and a style that combined a sure sense of scale and space, innovative planting decisions and astute selection of hard materials (all three qualities are present together only very rarely indeed at Chelsea). The Tom Stuart-Smith 'look' fitted the Chelsea environment perfectly, and he found himself catapulted into the garden-design arena. He would go on to create eight more gold-medal-winning gardens at Chelsea, three of which won the 'best in show' award. Never before or since has there been such an electrifying debut on the British garden-design scene. (John Brookes certainly caused a splash with his first Chelsea garden in 1962, but it didn't immediately translate into professional success as a designer.)

So, Tom left Elizabeth Banks Associates and joined Todd, Patrick James (another landscape architect) and architect Jamie Fobert (with whom he has collaborated several times) in an office near Tottenham Court Road in London – not as a formal partnership, but simply sharing office space. Ten years later Tom and Todd moved the shared office to London's Clerkenwell, and were joined by Jinny Blom; Tom says he enjoyed the loosely collaborative atmosphere, something he suggests he may have inherited from his father, who spent his early career working as a lawyer in chambers.

The projects in this book tell the story of the development of Tom's practice since that time. In addition, two essays by Tom himself reflect his thinking about landscape, which forms the background to his design decisions, and two by the author describe, first, Tom Stuart-Smith's planting methodology, and secondly his design philosophy.

The nurtured space

BROUGHTON GRANGE

SNOWDENHAM HOUSE

HOUSE IN KOTTAYAM

THE BARN

BROUGHTON GRANGE

BROUGHTON GRANGE

Previous pages
Spring tulips in the box parterre on the lower terrace.

Above
An early drawing made on trace paper, showing the terrace system and the pool at the heart of the design. This and the other drawn plans and sketches illustrated in this book are the work of the designer, who habitually creates a drawn overview of a planned garden before work commences on the ground.

Opposite
A rill of cut York stone leads to a tank on the middle terrace. The planting is dominated here by silvery *Stachys byzantina* and clumps of green-grey *Euphorbia nicaeensis*, with the seedheads of cardoon in the foreground.

This walled-garden project, in north Oxfordshire, has a special resonance for Tom because it was, as he says, 'the first big thing I did'. Commissioned in 2000, it was the garden that established Tom's style in the minds of the public and potential clients, an impression bolstered at that time and in ensuing years by a string of acclaimed Chelsea Flower Show gardens. 'In many ways I think this was the most important moment in my career,' Tom says, 'because it was the first big, constructed garden I made. It taught me so much about what was possible, and it sparked so many different thoughts as to what I could do.'

The site is roughly square, with a fall in level of around 3 metres (10 feet), its upper portion presenting views of the park and meadow all around. 'The genesis of this was definitely the client,' Tom recalls. 'He was talking to various people [i.e. other designers] and had a design on the back of an envelope. He had a six-acre field at his property and was envisaging a walled garden, enclosed on all sides. I looked at it and said, "You can't close these views off – they are just too good. Why don't we make a walled garden that is raised up, and make its greatest virtue the extent to which it is connected with its surroundings?"'

The result is a semi-walled garden (in that it has only two walls) consisting of three terraces, each with its own character. This was also an early collaboration with the architect Ptolemy Dean, who designed all the outbuildings and the principal garden walls. The terraces are flanked on one side by a beech tunnel and on the other by a trio of pleached lime-tree 'boxes'. On the top terrace sit two glasshouses, which help establish the underlying walled-garden theme, even if the overall

Left
Lime trees shade a walk along one edge of the terraces, with *Alchemilla mollis* and *Geranium* 'Patricia' below.

Opposite
The planting of the upper terrace includes blue-grey *Eryngium* x *zabelii* and crimson *Allium sphaerocephalon*, with columnar Irish yews lending structure.

impression is decidedly ornamental in character. Planting on this top terrace consists of generally quite low-growing 'Mediterranean' flowers and grasses, with shrubs planted only at the edges, so as not to impede the views. Multicoloured plantings of the likes of *Salvia* x *sylvestris* 'Blauhugel', *Achillea* 'Coronation Gold' and *Phlomis russeliana* are deployed in drifts, with sentinel Irish yews – which would become something of a trademark – creating height and a sense of structure.

'Why do I use fastigiate Irish yews so much?' Tom ponders. 'It's because I like the planting to be constantly changeable, and by contrast, there is something pretty strong, dominant and unchanging about the yews. It can be a little bit of a cheap trick, I suppose – but I don't think that is the case at Broughton because there is so much other material in there to disrupt their presence.'

As for the views beyond the garden, Tom explains that while certain elements of the landscape have influenced him, he has made no attempt to frame or capture specific vistas. 'I've never thought so much about what may be considered pictorial,' he explains. 'I think more about the thematic quality of the landscape.'

This was the first project where Tom used a geometric pool as the centrepiece of a design. In this case a narrow York stone rill flows directly down through the top terrace, the water then tumbling over a cascade and into a square tank on the middle terrace. The tank is 1 metre (3 feet) deep, which means that it is cool enough to contain fish (koi carp and sturgeon). The planting around it is more crowded than on the upper terrace, and has a damp meadow character, with persicarias, veronicastrums, phlox and tall grasses such as miscanthus species and *Calamagrostis* x *acutiflora* 'Karl Foerster'. The colours are richly burnished crimsons and golds, while uniform beech topiaries are dispersed across the piece.

The water tank feels like a void in the centre of the garden, an idea which Tom has reprised several times elsewhere, in different forms. 'I wanted the middle of the garden to feel empty, to be a centre you could not occupy,' he says. 'You cannot

stand there in the middle and say, "This was all made for me." So it's a garden with no resolution – it's all about the movement through it.'

The lowest section of the garden is a parterre of box hedges which are clipped just once a year to create a less formal aspect. The design was based on the microscopic cellular pattern of the leaves of native trees – beech, ash and oak – in the vicinity. The compartments created are filled with some 5,000 tulips in spring, followed by ornamental vegetables and annual flowers. Below here is another level, planted with large yew topiaries which have a sculptural presence akin to those found at gardens such as Levens Hall and Packwood House.

In many ways this garden is something of an extravaganza, as Tom readily admits. 'I was in a big "Eroica" phase at that time,' he reveals. 'I was obsessed by Beethoven (and Wagner – but we'll put him to one side). I wanted to do something that in winter was quite spartan and fairly tough, and then in summer emerged as something almost triumphant. This design is my "Eroica" moment. I look back on this and see it as a young man's garden, in that I probably couldn't do something as blatant as this now.'

Enlarging on this, Tom explains that he no longer feels the need 'to do a different thing on every terrace', and that topiary forms now play a more subdued role in his work. The echoes of the work of 1920s planting designer Norah Lindsay in his early work (rhythmic plantings below sentinel yews) have also subsided, while elements such as the stepping stones used in the pool here – almost an homage to Geoffrey Jellicoe's pool design at Sutton Place, a key modernist landscape statement – do not appear in later work.

This may be an 'early work' but Tom feels extremely warmly towards the garden. 'I still go there and I get a lot of joy out of seeing it,' he says. 'It's beautifully maintained and has great energy. That's a lovely thing to feel.'

Previous pages
The top terrace in winter, where the dead stems of miscanthus grasses are left to stand, along with (left) the dramatic 'candelabra' form of *Verbascum olympicum*.

Left
The lower terrace, with miscanthus in the foreground and the trees of the wider garden beyond.

Opposite
Frosted beech topiaries and Irish yews next to the rill.

SNOWDENHAM HOUSE

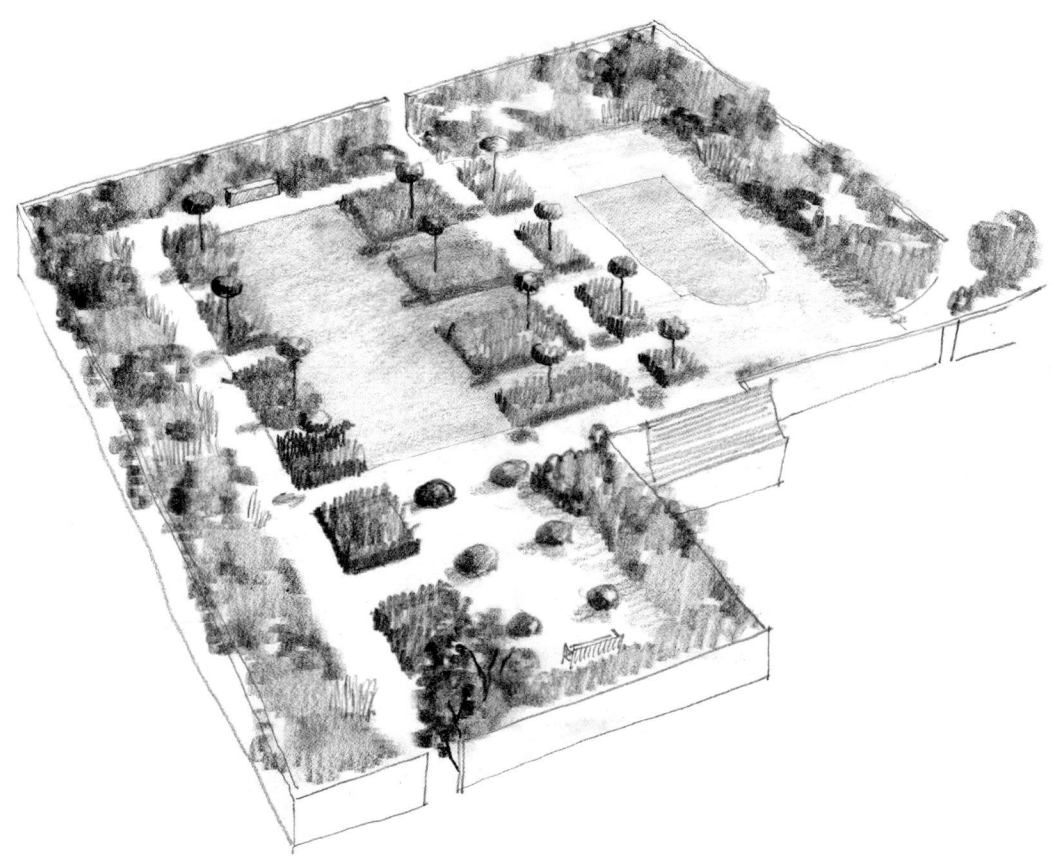

A jewel-like garden set around a swimming pool, occupying one enclosed section of an old walled garden in Surrey, this project does not have a philosophical or narrative programme like so many others in Tom's portfolio. Rather, it is a hedonistic space where the pool can be enjoyed amid attractive plantings which offer year-round interest. 'The owners are passionate gardeners and they wanted something quite horticulturally oriented,' Tom says. 'They do really look after that place.'

This is the smallest project, in terms of scale, in this book – but as his practice has developed Tom has remained keen on working with owners who demonstrate a real attachment to their garden.

Tom's plan was based on three rows of four *Parrotia persica* trees running parallel with the pool, with a lawn between the second and third rows, and underplantings in rectangular beds around each tree. The shape of the garden is what the owners describe as a 'wonky square', and to disguise the unorthodox dimensions, Tom organized the trees so that only the line closest to the pool is in fact straight. In addition, the planting beds beneath the trees are all of different sizes and taper in one direction, further enhancing the optical illusion.

These beds are repeat-planted with a palette of *Salvia nemorosa* 'Amethyst', *Amsonia hubrichtii* and *Geranium* 'Patricia', bolstered by perovskia, phlox, nepeta, astrantia and sedum, with the grasses *Stipa calamagrostis* and *Hakonechloa macra*. There is a diaphanous, delicate feel to the perennial composition, contrasting with the sturdy forms of the trees. The owners say that each of the *Parrotia* trees has its own character, and comment on the pleasure derived from swimming in the

Previous pages
A grove of parrotia trees next to the glass-tiled swimming pool.

Above
Preliminary sketch showing the irregular shape of the walled garden and the way the proposed ground plan helps to create the impression of regularity.

Opposite
Square beds beneath the trees contain plantings that include phlox, *Stipa calamagrostis* and *Euphorbia palustris*.

pool and looking up to see the undersides of the trees' leaves illuminated by the reflection of the water. Alliums have a strong presence – *A. cristophii* in spring and *A. sphaerocephalon* in July – together with tulips in four varieties: deep orange 'Abu Hassan', rich mauve 'Havran', vivid orange 'Ballerina' and crimson-and-yellow-striped 'Helmar'.

Tom replanted the beds on all four sides of the garden as a mixed border defined by shrubs including hydrangeas (*H. quercifolia*, *H. aspera* 'Villosa group'), *Schizophragma integrifolium* and *Trachelospermum jasminoides*, together with larger perennials including *Thalictrum delavayi*, *Eupatorium maculatum* 'Purple Bush', *Veronicastrum virginicum* and *Sanguisorba officinalis* 'Tanna'. In addition, a range of clematis ('Little Nell' and 'Étoile Violette') clamber up the walls, while thousands of snowdrops have been planted for winter interest.

The far (northeast) corner of the garden is the site of an old greenhouse and is the sunniest spot. It has been gravelled and given structure by means of a grid of clipped box balls, and is now gardened along Mediterranean lines – scillas, irises, chionodoxa and eryngiums pop up through the stones. A raised area in the corner, originally part of the greenhouse, has been planted with teucriums, sedums, galtonia, *Lotus hirsutus*, creeping rosemary and *Ozothamnus rosmarinifolius* 'Silver Jubilee', backed by purple-red *Clematis* 'Madame Julia Correvon'.

This is a felicitously scaled composition which is not overplanted – when that could have been the temptation. The parrotia trees lend a sense of unity and purpose to a garden of solid shapes and soft transparencies, best viewed from below ground level – while swimming the breaststroke perhaps.

Previous pages
A 'hot' corner of the garden, on the site of an old greenhouse, with the foliage of hellebores and purple *Hylotelephium telephium* 'Purple Emperor'.

Opposite
The path leading out to the main garden, with *Molinia* 'Transparent' (left) and *Echinacea purpurea* 'Magnus' (right).

Right
Purple phlox and perovskia with stipa grass under the shade of the parrotias.

HOUSE IN KOTTAYAM

HOUSE IN KOTTAYAM

The site of this project, at Kottayam in the southern Indian state of Kerala, was an old homestead set by a river in the coastal belt of waterways which is sandwiched between the Western Ghats and the Arabian Sea. 'The place was basically a derelict farm with a little old Keralan house up in the corner and lots of not very healthy trees – dying coconuts, mainly,' Tom recalls. 'It's about five miles from the setting of Arundhati Roy's novel *The God of Small Things*, which describes so vividly the heat, humidity and smells of fish, rotten mangoes and spices that fill the air in India so completely that sometimes there seems to be not enough space for oxygen.'

Tom's brief was to create a family garden with guest accommodation in this rural setting, while retaining something of the original farm-like atmosphere. 'Overall it is planted in the rural tradition,' he says. 'There is a banana grove, a coconut grove, and plantations of mangoes and mangosteens, cashews, cacao, pawpaws, betel nuts, bananas and so on. The only areas that are not planted with these crops are the vegetable garden in front of the house and the water tanks.'

Tom made two tanks, one large and one small, partly as a means of coping with monsoon flooding and partly for aesthetic reasons. 'The problem with this location is that the water-level difference is about ten to twelve feet between the rainy season and the rest of the year,' he explains. 'For part of the year, some of the site is underwater. The water tanks we made draw on the Indian tradition of tanks and step-wells in villages and holy places, and provides the only large open space on the site.'

The flooding issue meant that the first thing to be addressed was drainage. Most of the site was a bog during the rainy season, which was why the trees were failing.

Previous pages
Plantation trees such as mango, mangosteen and coconut surround the swimming pool and main house, with multi-stemmed frangipani on the terrace.

Above
Site sketch of the water tank in front of the main house, capturing some of the intended atmosphere.

Opposite
The landscape was organized as a series of plantations, in reference to the site's former identity as a working farm.

Previous pages
The central court of the main house in monsoon season.

Left
The garden's two water tanks, with a grass bridge between.

Opposite
The sculptural leaves of *Heliconia stricta* by the swimming pool.

Initially Tom's team tried to regulate the level in the water channels by building a lock on the main inflow from the river, but this was not successful because the water simply rose up out of the ground. Eventually, a workable drainage system was introduced, leaving 80 per cent of the area as moderately dry land (except at the height of the monsoon in June–July) and the rest as open water.

It was agreed early on that the farm should retain its productive aesthetic and that merely decorative plantings should be avoided, except in the immediate vicinity of the buildings. To this end Tom oversaw the establishment of an on-site nursery where plants – especially native ferns and gingers – were trialled for suitability. Areas around the house, in its courtyard, and along a new canal and the entrance drive were packed with tough plantings of species of *Heliconia, Alocasia, Colocasia, Hedychium*, ferns, leaf anthuriums, *Philodendron bipinnatifidum* and *Jasminum nitidum*. Many of these were native, and not all were readily identifiable; there is one specimen marked on Tom's office plans simply as 'local plant, similar to cosmos'.

A large, square vegetable garden was made in front of the old farmhouse using hand-cut basalt, and new staff quarters were placed behind this. The garden is arranged around these two opposing squares, with a new swimming pool and gym sandwiched between.

The local workforce was encouraged to deploy traditional working practices. 'The old-fashioned Indian way of doing this is much more ecological,' Tom says. 'All the plants are grown in coconut-fibre or terracotta pots. The planting team would arrive, we would do the setting-out of the plants in the afternoon, and they would plant just about all night by torchlight, to avoid the heat of the day.' In one large section of the garden, between the house and the river, Tom's team undertook no planting but simply edited what was already there. 'It was all about creating a management strategy and looking at the way local people work these farms,' Tom explains.

For this project, Tom collaborated with the architectural firm Studio Mumbai and its director Bijoy Jain. 'That was a big defining moment for me,' Tom recalls. 'At the point that I first met Jain he was running a studio of 20 architects, along with 60

carpenters and 80 masons in Alibag, just south of Mumbai. The working model is that much of the design work is done on site, which means that the designers learn as much from the craftsmen as the other way round. So when they build a project like this, the whole studio decamps en masse and lives on site. Quite often they undertake just one project at a time, so there is always a permanent site presence.'

'The carpenters were amazing,' Tom continues. 'Part of the process is the creation of beautiful, immaculate models made from old mahogany, where the trees are made of copper – exquisite. Then, when you move into the landscape they employ masons who have all the old traditional craft skills. It means you can go about the process in a way that is completely different from in the West. For example, building sites tend to be very quiet: all you can hear is the noise of the masons' hammers or the carpenters' handsaws. Things do take quite a long time to build. But virtually no concrete is used – it is all done with lime, almost like a medieval process. That's not an easy choice ... but it is a way of retaining a sense of closeness to nature. Things are made to fit around nature; existing trees are retained, growing right up close to the building. Jain thinks of buildings almost as animate beings. I find him such an interesting person to work with because it's all about the psychology of space, how you feel about it and respond to it, how it flows.'

Another key influence for Tom was Lunuganga in Bentota, Sri Lanka, the garden and house created by Geoffrey Bawa over a span of fifty years from the late 1940s. 'Much of the space around the buildings there is a little ambiguous,' Tom observes. 'Is it inside or outside? Is it a terrace or a path?' Tom says he has tried to introduce some of that fruitful ambiguity into this project.

'Despite the heat, the humidity and the curious travel arrangements,' he concludes, 'India is a wonderfully fulfilling and calming place to work, quite unlike anywhere else I've ever tried to make a garden. This is in part because you are so enveloped by the place – the heat, the humidity, the perfume, the lack of horizon, the constant presence of people.'

Previous pages
A glade of betel-nut and bananas helps retain the 'plantation' atmosphere.

Opposite
The main house, by Studio Mumbai, seen across the water tanks, which are designed to hold monsoon water.

Right
The main tank, with the pool building visible in the trees beyond.

THE BARN

Previous pages
The main garden at Tom Stuart-Smith's own home, planted as a 'continuum' with rhythmic plantings of the likes of macleaya (left) and orange-red *Helenium* 'Moerheim Beauty' (right).

Above
Drawn overview of the 'settlement' and landscape at the designer's home, showing Serge Hill House and gardens at right. The Barn sits at the centre, with the prairie garden to its left and the principal garden enclosures below it.

Opposite
Tall yellow verbascum and pale veronicastrum echo the verticals of the Irish yews.

Tom's own garden can be found across the lane from the 'big house' where he was brought up, at Serge Hill, in the Hertfordshire countryside 40 kilometres (25 miles) northwest of London. His grandfather bought the estate in 1926 and other family members still live there, but Tom was drawn to a fine old barn which he remembered playing in as a child. This is now his living room, with an impressive vaulted roof of timber beams, since it was converted into a house in 1986–87.

The garden functions as a place for experimentation and also as somewhere he can take pleasure in gardening himself. 'It's a playground,' he says. 'I can make impulsive decisions, never plan, make mistakes, rootle around, and generally not be too organized.' But the garden plays a deeper role, too. For Tom, there has always been a palpable division between the active and the contemplative life; his own garden is a place where he can throw himself into physical activity at weekends.

The first evidence of gardening at The Barn is a sunken courtyard – originally the farmyard – that prefaces the barn and its one-storey extensions, which semi-enclose the space on three sides. This was initially designed with formal hedges, almost as a knot garden, but was completely revamped in 2007 using the Corten steel water tanks deployed in Tom's Chelsea Flower Show garden of the previous year. The linear plan is simple, with the tanks brimful with reflective water, while the planting is colourful and complex. The Corten is a resolutely modern material, but it recalls 'the rusty past of the farmyard', as Tom puts it.

'Modernism is so often connected with minimalism in garden design,' he says. 'Planting gets reduced to monocultures or tasteful combinations of "plant material"

that complement rather than contrast. I wanted to make a garden that was all about contrast – between a garden plan that was so simple it was almost mundane, and a content that was full of texture, detail and colour.' Large numbers of bearded irises dominate in early summer, with astrantias, *Euphorbia margalidiana*, *Salvia nemorosa* 'Ostfriesland', *Hylotelephium* 'Matrona' and the grasses *Hakonechloa* and *Anemanthele lessoniana* (which tinges red and orange in autumn). Later the brooms come into their own, along with panicum grasses, eryngiums, achilleas, echinaceas and coreopsis.

Tom summarizes the structure of the main garden, behind the barn, as 'four semi-enclosed spaces that are full of plants and two enclosed spaces that are empty green rooms'. These spaces have been created by hedges of yew (nearer the house) and hornbeam, planted during the early 1990s. From a small terrace a straight vista speeds westwards over a rectangular panel of lawn flanked by a pair of short but deep borders and on to a tall, clipped hornbeam hedge complex, pierced to allow for the vista to continue along a mown path through meadow beyond, before dissolving into woodland.

The planting design is, as Tom describes, on 'a gradient of naturalism' as one moves further from the house, from the slightly more decorative – 'dahlias, penstemons, the occasional sunflower or other annual, and the odd climbing rose' – to a more meadowy planting, where the colour range is blue, purple and yellow, with less rich red and bronze. Self-seeding wild plants are permitted towards the fringes – wild carrot, foxgloves and scabious ('if it is a good one').

Grasses now make up a quarter of the planting scheme, while another key emphasis is on the tall perennials which Tom often uses in his professional work: veronicastrums, *Macleaya*, cardoons, vernonia, species hollyhocks and *Helianthus*. He particularly values the translucent delicacy of *Thalictrum delavayi* and *Cephalaria dipsacoides* among these more strident characters, and *Dianthus carthusianorum* performs a similar function at a lower level. Defining plants of

Previous pages
The prairie in late summer creates a setting and counterpoint to the main garden spaces, which are more formal in style.

Left
The hornbeam enclosure at the heart of the garden, showing the browsing line and path taken by muntjac deer.

Opposite
At the edges of the garden the planting composition becomes much looser, given definition here by the spikes of foxtail lilies (*Eremurus*).

Previous pages
The main vista due west from the barn terrace, with *Stipa calamagrostis* grasses and (at left) *Geranium* 'Patricia'.

Left
The vegetable garden, with tulips and hazel-work. This part of the garden has been extended and is very much the domain of Sue Stuart-Smith.

spring and early summer are foxtail lilies (the white *Eremurus* 'Joanna') and giant fennel, while large clumps of the yellow daisy *Inula racemosa* emerge as a strong presence. As summer progresses the spires of the hollyhocks and verbascums appear, 'like the spires of the City churches in 18th-century views of London'.

Texture and form are of more importance to Tom than flower colour, and to that end he favours plants with 'real backbone and distinctive foliage' – euphorbias, eupatoriums, veronicastrums and silphium in repeated groups to create a rhythmic simplicity. Of the smaller perennial plants, Tom has come to particularly value the amsonias – 'I am yet to find one that isn't worth growing'. Repetition is key, with sedums, euphorbias, salvias, calamagrostis, miscanthus (mainly *M. sinensis* 'Malepartus') and clary sage cropping up everywhere, while masses of cranesbill geraniums provide low-level structure.

It was not always like this. 'I grew roses for years and I used to spray them,' Tom recalls. 'But we were fighting a losing battle. So I thought, why not give that up entirely and just do one thing – make a place that is possessed of a slowly shifting atmosphere. It's much more interesting to have a feeling of continuity, a sense that you are drifting from space to space.' As such, this is not a garden with a beginning, a middle and an end, a sequential experience of contrasting spaces in the Arts and Crafts manner. It operates more as a tone poem, its varied moods and moments always unified by an all-pervading rhythm. This is immersive continuum planting in the modern style, possessed of form, texture and rhythm, but with none of the colour theory of an older, 20th-century tradition.

In 2011 Tom began an experimental 'exotic prairie' with his regular collaborator, naturalistic planting researcher James Hitchmough. This pushes the theme even further, since the rationale is simply to disperse seed mixes across the space and wait to see what happens. The plant mix includes silphium, baptisia, echinaceas, *Coreopsis tripteris*, *Lobelia tupa* and silene, with *Rudbeckia fulgida* var. *deamii* and asters dominating later in the season. It stands at one remove from the rest of the garden, and comes as a surprise and a delight.

PLANTING

Tim Richardson

For many people with an interest in gardens and landscape design, the first image which springs to mind when Tom Stuart-Smith's name is mentioned is his planting style – exuberant, large-scale naturalistic design using mainly herbaceous perennials, organized in rhythmic swathes or drifts which form a continuum across the garden space. Tom's intention is generally to create a transcendent, timeless experience, where certain motifs commence and recur, surging and receding with the seasons so that there seems to be no beginning, middle or end to the experience. Tom favours musical analogies to describe the effect of these plantings, with different themes or ideas appearing, combining and repeating in real time like the subjects in a Bach fugue.

In common with many other designers of his generation, Tom has been decisively influenced by the naturalistic turn in planting design across Europe (and increasingly America) since the mid-1990s, and he has collaborated with several other leading figures in this milieu including Piet Oudolf, James Hitchmough and Nigel Dunnett. Not so much a design trend as a cultural phenomenon, the naturalistic planting movement echoes growing public awareness of ecology and human responsibility for the planet. It is likely that it will continue to be a leitmotif in garden-making well into the middle of this century.

Broadly speaking, Tom's is an immersive as opposed to a pictorial style (the latter being the traditional Arts and Crafts manner). Plants are not organized as set-piece features such as long borders or single-species gardens, or according to colour theory, but are instead considered to be materials that can be harnessed to create a sense of a seamless composition that pervades the whole garden space. The rhythm of the garden is therefore dictated at least as much by the planting regimen as by the spaces and episodes which constitute its formal structure. Of his own garden at The Barn, Tom says: 'I never think of these spaces as rooms. I like everything to interconnect: one overall story, with a series of subplots, not a series of episodes. I want the whole garden to be one malleable entity.'

While the naturalistic or 'New Perennials' planting movement can be described as internationalist in spirit, there are certain traits or habits of mind peculiar to British designers which tend to give their work in this mode a rather different texture from what one may find in Germany or the Netherlands.

An experience I had while touring gardens in the Netherlands during this book's preparation neatly illustrates this point. After several days of visiting designed gardens, I found myself looking at yet another border made up of exactly the same plant varieties. I mentioned to the designer-owner of the garden that I felt I had been looking at these same plants in several different gardens over the past week, and then name-checked the specific dozen or so over-familiar grasses and perennials on view. The Dutch designer responded, 'Yes, they are great plants, aren't they?' There was no sense of irony in that reply, nor any sign that the implicit criticism of my question had been registered. A typical British gardener or designer, by contrast, would have been mortified, since the garden culture of the UK is highly competitive and traditionally fixated on constant horticultural innovation (which is, after all, the prime theme of Chelsea Flower Show and all the other British garden shows).

This is not a criticism, per se, but a (horti-)cultural observation, a sidelight on Tom Stuart-Smith's own background as a British gardener and designer. He does use some of the same plants as in those Dutch gardens, but they form part of a more complex plant palette. Individual varieties would certainly be dropped if they started to appear over-used or clichéd – the cow parsley *Ammi majus* and spindly *Verbena bonariensis* have certainly fallen into this category in recent years, perhaps soon to be followed by *Cephalaria gigantea* and *Stipa gigantea.* Of his own garden, Tom observes: 'The garden is stuffed with plants, it's true – but I hope people don't just come and gawp at the flowers. I hope they will see the spatial progression and above all how the centre is related to the periphery, and then how the whole relates to the landscape surrounding it.'

Notwithstanding such observations, Tom can most certainly be described as a plantsman who has developed his own horticultural methodology. 'I think that texture, for me, is most important,' he begins.

I very rarely use spiky, hard plants like yuccas, phormiums or mahonias, except in hot countries where they are more the norm. I always think

Design for the Hepworth Wakefield Garden, 2018.

Design drawing for a garden for Laurent-Perrier, Chelsea Flower Show, 2008.

about contrasts in texture, shades of green, size of leaf and reflectivity (whether leaves are glossy or matt or hairy) before I think about colour. For example, at home I have a lot of [the daisy-flowered] *Inula magnifica* 'Sonnenstrahl', used as much for its magnificent leaves and the contrast they make with diaphanous things like *Stipa gigantea*, *Cenolophium denudatum* and *Althaea cannabina*. I think about contrasts in movement and transparency/solidity a good deal, also. Grasses are the key to movement: miscanthus are such wonderful accompaniments to big clumps of *Eupatorium maculatum* – the vertical line and the horizontal, the more mobile with the static.

Perhaps first of all, when it comes to planting, I think about character and mood. Mood might sometimes almost mean 'mode' – are we in Arts and Crafts roses-and-delphinium mode, or in an organized linear border, or is it something more wild, unbuttoned and three-dimensional? Of course, this last choice is most fashionable at the moment and perhaps also the most immersive, but the other approaches very much have their place in the right context. Different rules apply to each. For example, when in full-on nostalgia mode I am very happy to use highly bred plants, more clumped and defined, with the gaps between occupied by more ephemeral things like Miss Willmott's Ghost [*Eryngium giganteum*], hesperis or foxgloves.

One of Tom's peculiarities as a planting designer is his willingness and ability to mingle traditional English 'cottage-garden' flowers, such as phlox and geraniums, with plants that are more associated with the New Perennials palette – large things such as veronicastrum, eupatorium and thalictrum.

Tom is prepared to push the analogy even further:

I think that there is a lot to be said for having almost archetypal models in the back of your mind. Like the orchard filled with cow parsley, or the bluebell wood. Even if it's only as a partial model – for instance, a grove of cornus underplanted with camassias has the scale of hazel coppice. It's a spatial language we are familiar with on some deeper level. Sometimes there can be quite oblique

Design drawing for the entrance garden, RHS Bridgewater, 2018, based on a Voronoi diagram, a mesh-like pattern found in organic forms (such as a giraffe's hide).

or very light references back to these kinds of ideas. It can add an element of subtle reference that you don't necessarily pick up on explicitly at the time, but it gives the setting an aura of inexplicable familiarity.

Another planting method that Tom uses in most of his projects, and that lends many of his gardens their particular texture and atmosphere, is the concept of a 'float' planting of low-growing, textural plants that can self-seed across a whole garden or garden area – plants such amsonia, gillenia or astrantia, to name just a handful. Tom's planting plans typically include a list of five or six of these 'float' plants, liberally deployed across the whole design. At the project entitled in this book 'A Garden in the Surrey Hills'(for reasons of privacy) they include *Gaura lindheimeri*, *Verbascum bombyciferum* 'Arctic Summer' and *Lilium* 'Citronella'. Certain plants here also provide rhythmic links, notably *Cephalaria gigantea*, *Veronicastrum virginicum* 'Fascination', *Miscanthus sinensis* 'Malepartus', *Echinacea pallida* and different species of thalictrum, while other plants, such as *Cynara cardunculus* act more as 'accents'. Overall this scheme is based on light blues and soft purples, with the judicious addition of yellow from the likes of *Phlomis russeliana*. 'I want that border – and the whole garden – to get quite shaggy over time,' Tom says. 'I showed the clients photographs of Waltham Place [the Berkshire garden designed by Henk Gerritsen] to illustrate that idea of slight abandonment.'

A criticism that is occasionally levelled against Stuart-Smith is that his gardens look too similar, that he 'rolls out' his projects according to a pre-established horticultural template. This is a superficial observation, as the wide range of designs in this book demonstrates. On the other hand, in common with most garden designers working at the highest level, Tom does favour certain reliable plants which he returns to time and again, and which can appear prominent in photographs taken for magazine articles at a particular moment of the season (usually late summer). In this context, Tom mentions that he learnt something early on from Piet Oudolf, whom he cites as a major influence: 'I remember

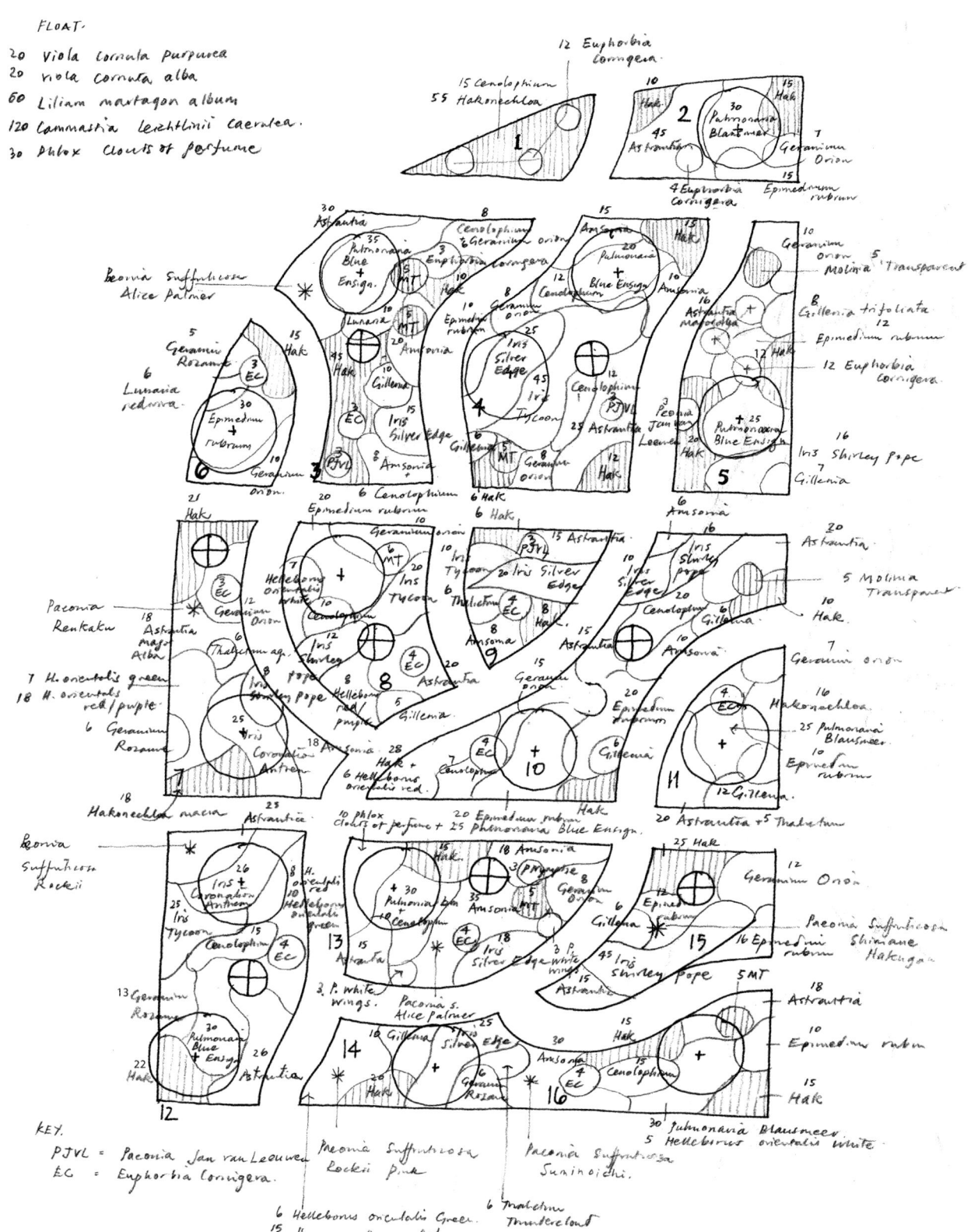

Planting plan for part of the walled garden at Culham Court, intended to look its best in spring and early summer. Grasses are shown with vertical hatching.

having a conversation with Piet about fifteen years ago, about how you might approach a job,' he says. 'And I just said gaily that when I did Broughton Grange, I made a plant schedule for each part of the garden and then made it up as I went along. But then Piet said, in a very nice way, that I was mad – that this approach was fine if you only have one job, and you have loads of time to spend on it. But that you will find over time, when you have lots of other projects to work on, that perhaps the most important thing of all is the ability to learn from your own work. And that the only way you can do that is if you codify it and then come back and see what has happened over time.'

To demonstrate the point, Tom recalls 'going to see Pensthorpe [Oudolf's project in Norfolk] six years after it was planted. All the laminated planting plans were still there, and it was pretty much as per the plan. That is what is so brilliant about Piet – he is like a composer, in that more than anybody else in the world he has codified beauty, in a way, and learnt how to abstract it on to a page. Whereas most people are not really there – they are probably making it up a little, on the hoof, on the ground. They know what will work when they're planting it, but they are not actually writing it out as a script which can be referred to in future. That is how I try to work now.'

Tom's planting at Broughton was one example of his approach in action:

> I wanted to be involved as closely as possible in the process of making it so I made lists for each part of the garden and then laid it out on site. The areas of planting, dominated by herbaceous plants, were big, generally between 100 and 200 sq. m [1,000–2,150 sq. ft] and were composed into three terraces stepping down into the landscape. The upper terrace is the hottest and driest and is planted with an intricate tapestry of Mediterranean, drought-tolerant plants including cistus, genista, phlomis and a complex of perennials such as salvias, eryngiums, euphorbias and grasses. There is a rectilinear arrangement of paths around the garden and then smaller informal paths through the planting connecting these, but these smaller winding paths are not apparent at first glance. You have to get among

Planting plan of the middle terrace at Mount St John. Three beds about 12 metres (40 feet) square are dotted with low box domes, with a narrow winding path weaving across.

Constantinsborg, Denmark: sketch of a proposal for part of the garden, showing a mix of wild flowers, flowering trees and topiary framing a pre-existing formal parterre, 2019.

it all to see. On the middle terrace the planting is much more luxuriant and is based on the idea of a damp meadow, with much bolder clumps: rodgersia, veronicastrum and phlox, contrasting with tall grasses which weave through a loose pattern of clipped beech shapes. My intention was to base the planting on each terrace loosely on a specific type of plant community. I altered the soil to suit the plant content, making the top terrace more free draining by adding quantities of grit and the middle terrace more moisture-retentive and fertile by adding farmyard manure. I chose a palette of plants that suited the kind of atmosphere I wanted to create: more lean, tight and wiry on the upper terrace with a good deal of intermingling; more lush and bold on the middle terrace. Above all, I wanted to create an irrepressible sense of abundance and energy in contrast to the quite rigid and crystalline structure of the garden. I always put texture and form before colour, thinking about juxtapositions of gloss against matt, fine against coarse, smooth against ridged. Fifteen years on I regret both that

I made no plan to monitor the changes in the garden and that I used so many self-seeding plants. This gave the garden a great spontaneity and vigour, although in some years it veers a little off piste.

Tom has also had to work with unfamiliar plant palettes when designing gardens in countries beyond the UK. In these projects, as he admits, the challenge of using exotic plant materials, when most of his knowledge is based on temperate plants, has been greatly eased by local nurserymen who have helped him to get to grips with the local vegetation. At Kottayam in Kerala, Le Jardin Secret in Marrakech and more recently La Granja Alnardo in Spain, he has concentrated on using native plants as well as, where possible, indigenous ideas about how land is cultivated and perceived.

To place Tom's work in context, it might be observed that there are two dominant strands to the naturalistic planting movement as it has developed over the past few decades. The first is scientific in flavour, with an emphasis on horticultural experimentation to identify plants which can be used particularly in public planting schemes. The idea of 'design' is downplayed and terms such as 'matrix planting' are deployed by the botanical researchers – as they are known – working in this field, notably the 'Sheffield School' led by James Hitchmough at the university in that city in northern England. The second strand is more artistically nuanced, and is essentially a continuation of the 'wild-garden' theories of the late 19th-century plantsman William Robinson, who stipulated that any plant might be used in any context, as long as it is aesthetically justified and looks 'natural' in its environment. From the evidence of the projects highlighted in this book, it is clear that Tom has been drawn to both approaches at different times and in different contexts.

A fruitful 'middle way' between these opposing attitudes might be found at his scheme for La Granja Alnardo. Here, Tom and his client have made discriminatory aesthetic choices about the plantings (which are not confined to natives), and then about the management or 'editing' of the vegetation as it appears. Overall, however, they have tried to let the plantings develop in as uninhibited a way as possible, so that they colonize not only the environs of the property, but then also merge with the surrounding natural landscape and its flora. 'I'm increasingly interested in creating gardens that can be managed rather than gardened,' Tom says. 'Working with Piet

A design drawing for a stream garden in Surrey, not carried out.

Oudolf has taught me how he is amazingly good at producing a something with a naturalistic look, but which is also incredibly structural and manageable.'

A similar approach was adopted by Tom in designing Vergelegen, a project around a very modern and uncompromising house in Massachusetts, USA, set in a seemingly wild landscape of rolling, wooded country. As he describes: 'All the planting is of native plants, so there isn't a hiatus between the cultivated and the natural. In the undercroft of the house we used local ferns and sedges. In the open ground beyond the house we exposed areas of rocky outcrop.' In addition, 4 hectares (10 acres) were sown as prairie 'so the design emphasizes an unfiltered confrontation between grand wildness of the landscape on the one hand and the house on the other'.

Tom is more committed to this approach – and further ahead – than many. There can be an element of paying lip service to such ideas in the profession at large, which is understandable because it is a high-risk strategy: the plant community observed, replicated and then dispersed as seed on a site may not turn out to be anything like expected in its new situation. It might even fail. Tom has learnt that clients have to be just as committed to the approach as the practitioner, accepting that complete or partial failure can be an intrinsic aspect of experimentation.

It's an idea Tom has been developing for several years in other projects, and it has particular resonance with regard to the increasing naturalism of his planting designs. Of his own garden at The Barn he has written: 'In recent years I have come to see the garden less as a series of events and more as part of a place in the landscape, an intermediary between the barn and the wider setting.'

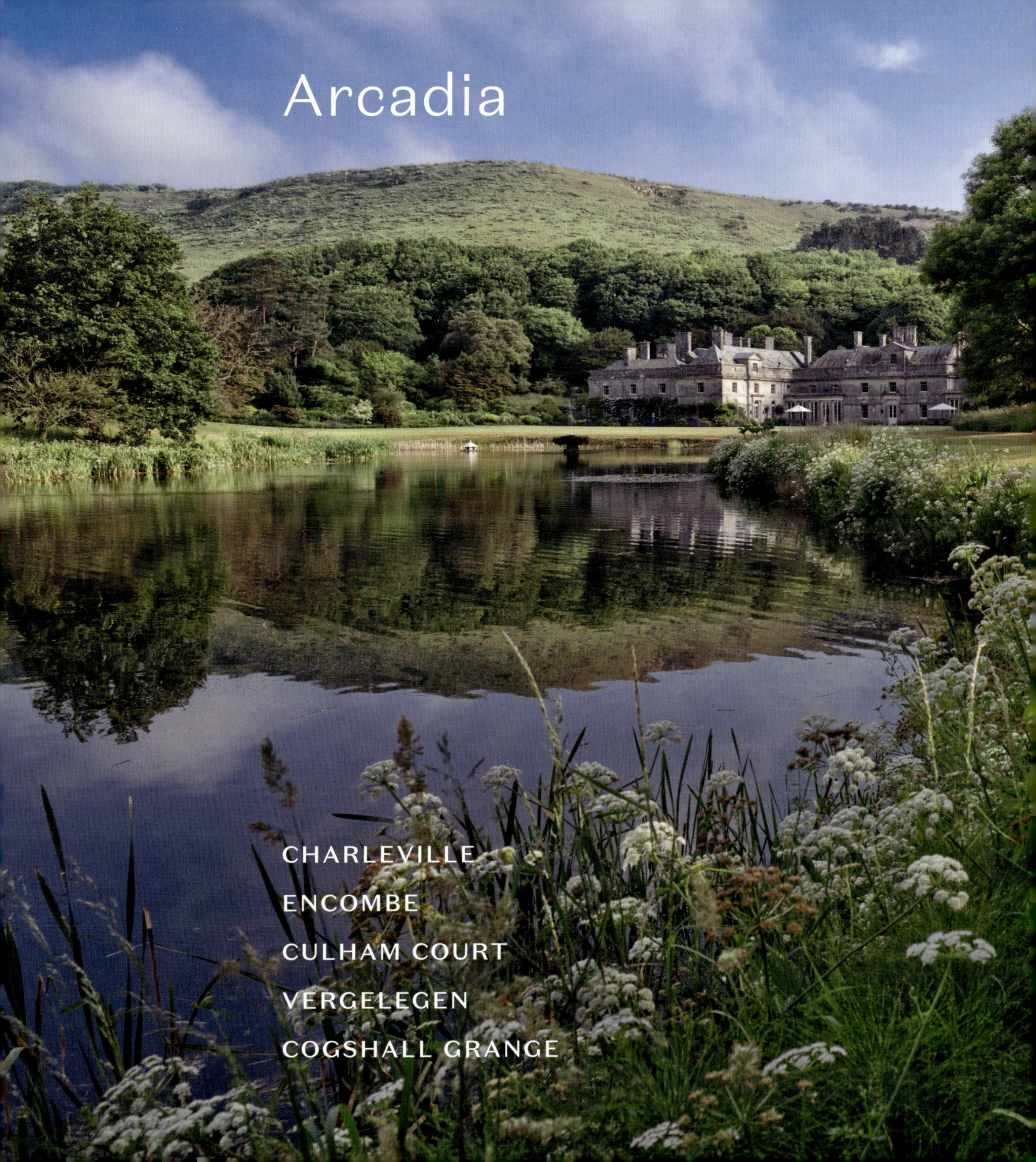

Arcadia

CHARLEVILLE

ENCOMBE

CULHAM COURT

VERGELEGEN

COGSHALL GRANGE

CHARLEVILLE

Previous pages
Yew pyramids and hakonechloa grass are the constituent parts of the Nut Grove, a garden 'room' that Tom designed as a palette cleanser.

Above
The drawing for the Nut Grove, with clipped yew pyramids set amid grasses.

Opposite
The walled garden is made up of large, box-hedged planting beds filled with shrub roses and supporting shrubs such as *Hoheria* (against the wall).

Sometimes a designer will want to pursue a 'scorched-earth' policy at a new project, completely removing what was there before. But on other occasions, and particularly at historic properties, a lighter touch is desirable. This has been Tom's approach at several important commissions – at Fort Belvedere, for example, and also at Charleville, in Co. Wicklow, about 25 kilometres (15 miles) south of Dublin. The estate of some 162 hectares (400 acres) includes 12 hectares (30 acres) of garden, most of which is an ornamental parkland setting for specimen trees, stands of pine and avenues of yew, holly and other species, each of which forms its own shape and casts its own shadow-colour. Shallow flights of steps, high hedges, smooth lawns, urns and statues help create a Tennysonian atmosphere in this wider setting: a suspension of time and space.

The walled garden, to the west of the house, is the focus for decorative horticulture, which is taken extremely seriously at Charleville. Tom has edited and made additions to the flower borders and also added a few new enclosed garden areas, but he has left the path layout and many of the plantings almost intact.

'It's a very valuable garden to me and a place where I love going – because we have done everything very slowly,' Tom says. 'I go there without fail once a year. We have done one project, or perhaps half a project, each year for something like fifteen years. It's a continuing conversation with the clients.'

Typically, Tom views the situation in its historical context: 'I remember walking around St Paul's Walden Bury [in Hertfordshire] with [the landscape designer] Geoffrey Jellicoe. He had been going there for many years and worked with two generations of the same family. You couldn't help looking at him as a sort of

Left
A quartet of tall yew pyramids plays its role in this highly structured garden. The birch *Betula ermanii* can be seen in the background.

Opposite
Within the tight structure, an informal woodland feel is created, with winding paths leading through the likes of purple-red *Cirsium rivulare* 'Atropurpureum', ferns, darmera and *Selinum wallichianum* (milk parsley).

guardian of the place, in that he could see things that others couldn't. I am now sufficiently old that I have one or two gardens where I have worked for the parents and then the next generation. It's an amazing thing, to have such a long-term connection with a place.'

The essential tone of the garden at Charleville is classic Arts and Crafts, with numerous shrub roses in herbaceous borders across the garden, along with cottage flowers such as delphiniums. Tom admits that this is not his natural style, but he has made a decision to work alongside it. 'It's about accommodating your own style to other people's tastes and the existing tone,' he explains. 'I find that it's almost a sociological experiment to try to adapt your planting style to a historical precedent.'

The walled garden at Charleville takes the form of a stained-glass window. The semicircular northern end is a velvety lawn flanked by intense areas of planting contained by luxuriantly curved low box hedging, while the lower part of the garden is made up of six separate enclosed areas.

In the planting beds Tom has retained some plants, such as inula, ligularia, monarda and crocosmia, while adding others in rhythmic fashion, for a subtle modernizing influence, including *Helenium* 'Rubinzverg', *Rudbeckia maxima* and *Miscanthus sinensis* 'Malepartus'. The existing romantic palette also included roses, lupins, astrantias, cornus, cardoons, campanulas, peonies, acanthus and dahlias. There is a sense that Tom has retained some of these slightly through gritted teeth: 'I'm not easy about having old-fashioned David Austin roses mixed up in the borders,' he says. 'Unless they are wild species roses, my feeling is that roses belong in a rose garden.' But Tom relented because the clients love roses and are in residence only from April to August. Delphiniums were another species that posed a challenge. 'The problem with delphiniums is they are such show-stealers,' he says. 'They don't really mingle. As a compromise I always use soft-coloured varieties.'

A venerable conservatory sits in the centre of the garden, with a line of 52 flask-shaped yews running south across a large, informal lawn area with mature trees. On the north side is an apsidal fountain garden, with statues arranged in recesses set in a yew hedge, reminiscent of the exedra at Chiswick House, west London. Tom added some box plants in terracotta pots to help with the scale and proportion of the space.

On the western edge of the walled garden is an historic beech tunnel, with two enclosed areas adjacent to it designed by Tom. The rose garden is an intensely romantic space, with roses grown as both shrubs and standards, as well as on swags on the east side. It was important to Tom that a perennial layer was included – 'I hate the idea of a rose garden without plants on the ground' – so various other flowers also play a role here: astrantias 'Roma' and 'Claret', *Geranium* 'Rozanne', nepeta, amsonia, stachys and epimediums. A central font is surrounded by lavender and thyme.

South of this is a garden which Tom originally conceived as a nuttery, centred on a bronze statue of a female figure in Art Nouveau style. In the event, the garden takes the form of yew pyramids set in a sea of hakonechloa grass (some 5,000 individual plants), which rustle in the wind. It's a simple and elegant conceit. 'I wanted something which was an absolute counterpoint to the over-the-top nature of the rose garden,' Tom says. 'It was just the idea of a breathing space. I felt that if you had another highly ornamental garden the whole thing would be indigestible.' The southernmost part of the walled garden is an orchard divided into two sections planted with Nigel Dunnett's 'Pictorial Meadows' mixes of annual flowers: 'Pastel' to the west ('strawberries and cream'), and 'Aqua' to the east (blue and magenta).

In a way, Tom's task at Charleville is an object lesson in knowing when not to do things, as well as when to intervene. 'It's about continuity versus change, and about the virtues of a long game,' he reflects. 'If you are going to turn something like that around, it can take a long time.'

Previous pages
An unburdened feel in the borders, with foxgloves growing around *Rosa glauca* and (front left) *Geranium psilostemon* with *Allium cristophii*.

Opposite
The flowers, stems and leaves of *Rodgersia pinnata* cascade over a path in the walled garden.

Right
The terrace by the house, with box in pots on the steps, giving way to lawns and parkland.

ENCOMBE

Previous pages
The low-slung Palladian house in its valley setting.

Above
A drawing of the south front of the house, looking out over the lake.

Opposite
Roses and a wide range of plants in pots cluster around the door which leads directly to the garden.

'I have been to few places where the arrival has been so emotionally overpowering – Encombe is the nearest thing to entering Narnia.' That was Tom's initial comment on this 1,000-hectare (2,500-acre) estate which occupies a superbly privileged position on the Dorset coast. He continues: 'The experience of driving over the crest of the hill as one enters the estate and then descending to the heart of this island of green is like a journey into the deepest recesses of consciousness, where what is barely discernible is revealed gradually and the entire composition builds in intensity as the centre is approached … It is hard to think of an historic designed landscape in Britain with greater natural drama and beauty than Encombe. Its position, sandwiched between the Purbeck Hills and the sea, gives it a special quality of separateness so that one has the impression … that you are somewhere quite apart from the rest of England.'

This is no exaggeration – the low-slung, early 18th-century neoclassical mansion looks out across a large artificial 'infinity lake' which appears to meld with the misty sea beyond, the views framed by strategically placed trees and the enfolding contours of the land. There are woodland walks with artificial cascades and high-level rides across the thrilling coastal topography (Encombe boasts its own beach), as well as a grotto, 'rocky bridge', classical temple and once a large rotunda (now vanished). Finally, a delightfully topsy-turvy walled garden is pocketed in among a collection of hills and hummocks. The estate as a whole has a markedly fluid feel to it, as if it is constantly moving around you – almost like the sea itself.

The house and designed landscape visible today were mainly the work of John Pitt, who lived at Encombe from 1734 until his death in 1787. Pitt was a connoisseur

Previous pages
The hedged 'paradise garden' sits in the midst of the walled garden, with the white spires of *Eremurus* 'Joanna' singing out.

Opposite
Most of the walled garden is taken up by orchard trees in a meadow setting, with oxeye daisy dominant.

Right
The path that leads to the temple, with Siberian irises and pink *Paeonia lactiflora* 'Nymphe'.

of art and gardens and a member of the Society of Dilettanti. He designed several garden buildings for Lord Lyttelton at Hagley Park, Worcestershire, one of the most famed landscape gardens of the day. It has been suggested that Willam Pitt the Elder, a famous relative, designed parts of Encombe, but historical analysis indicates that it was probably all the work of John Pitt.

Tom was commissioned to work across the whole estate in 2010, shortly after it had been taken on by new owners. When he arrived, the courtyard against the south front of the house (the original entrance) was occupied by a sunken croquet lawn, interrupting views out across the lake towards the sea. 'It was pretty austere before,' Tom comments. 'It wasn't a house where you stepped out into the landscape.' The croquet lawn was replaced by a sleek terrace of Purbeck stone, framed by substantial plantings against the house. These must be tough and vigorous in the exposed coastal situation – roses including 'Aimée Vibert' and 'Francis E. Lester' flourish alongside grapevines, *Melianthus major*, rosemary, eupatoriums and *Euphorbia* x *pasteurii*.

The landscape around the lake itself has been transformed by the removal of post-and-rail fencing which previously created a series of paddocks. The lake's pristine setting has been recovered, at the same time reintroducing a sense of connection with the high hills on both sides of the combe as it descends to the sea. A lot of thought and work has gone into making this connection between garden and landscape more seamless.

This idea of the rhythm of the landscape was extended to encompass the classical temple, a mid-19th-century addition set on rising ground to the southwest. 'I felt there was too direct a connection between the temple and the house,' Tom explains. The solution was to introduce new twin shrubberies on either side of the building, so that it now is more screened and can be discovered as a surprise. The shrubberies contain big plantings of sanguisorba, persicaria, *Euphorbia* x *pasteurii*

and grasses (molinia and hakonechloa) set around cloud-formed box clumps and masses of sweet-scented sarcococca. Old pines, yews and oaks tower above younger plantings of cornus and acers, while in spring *Narcissus* 'Thalia' lights up the grassy banks below the temple. The southern shrubbery has a slightly darker, moodier feel, with shrubs such as *Viburnum cinnamomifolium* adding to the atmosphere.

The temple and its shrubberies are a staging post on the short journey towards the separate walled garden, which Tom thinks of as the heart of the estate: 'I got fixated on this idea of the omphalos, the navel of the world,' he says. 'It was all about the Russian doll character of the place: a garden within a wall within a pleasure ground within a park within a valley within an island.' The idea is expressed as a small, yew-hedged enclosure in the centre of the space. It is maintained as a jewel-like paradise garden surrounded by an orchard of apple, pear, plum, quince and gage trees, all set in a wildflower meadow, where masses of camassias and *Gladiolus byzantinus* come up in springtime.

The hedged central garden is a dreamlike space filled with climbing roses ('Madame Alfred Carrière', 'Cécile Brunner') on metal arches and supports, and adorned by yew obelisks. A quartet of arbours, one at each corner, is festooned with espaliered apple 'Tydeman's Late Orange'. The planting is rich and romantic, with the red tree peony *Paeonia delavayi* used as a link plant amid geraniums, eremurus, gaura, philadelphus, salvias and nepeta.

All four inner walls of the main walled garden are intensively gardened with shrubs, perennials and grasses, while perched above on its north side is a rectangular productive garden, where yew buttresses mark out beds for vegetables and cut flowers, as well as cold frames, a fruit cage and glasshouse. From this vantage point, the landscape can be properly appreciated, seemingly ebbing and flowing in all directions. As the head gardener points out: there are no straight lines at Encombe.

Previous pages
Inside the paradise garden, with roses, eremurus, the grass *Stipa tenuissima* and the small purple-red flowers of *Dianthus carthusianorum*.

Left
A stand of high-pruned *Quercus ilex* is carefully managed so as to frame views in both directions.

Opposite
A specimen of *Rosa nutkana* 'Plena' stands out in the shrubbery by the temple.

CULHAM COURT

CULHAM COURT

Previous pages
The central pool in the walled garden, with crab apples, box topiary and panicum grass.

Above
Design drawing for the walled garden, depicting its tripartite structure, the long narrow pool at the centre and the 'slip garden' for fruit, vegetables and cut flowers in the triangular space nearest to the viewer.

Opposite
Bupleurum fruticosum around a door to the walled garden. The paths are made of Flemish bricks laid on edge.

The stretch of the River Thames at Hambleden, a few miles downstream from Henley, is one of the loveliest in the valley, as the river describes an elegant (almost) hairpin bend, with the valley sides clothed with green fields and small parcels of woodland. Perhaps the best spot of all, on the south (Berkshire) bank, was chosen in the medieval period as the site of Culham Court, though the current house, by William Chambers, was built in 1771. The estate still encompasses some 1,400 hectares (3,500 acres), including rolling parkland grazed by a herd of white fallow deer, scions of royal Danish stock.

In 2010 Tom was asked by new owners to revamp the terraces in front of the house, looking over the Thames far below, and also the immediate environs of the house, which is quite starkly set on the lip of the valley. But his most important contribution was a new design for the walled garden, downhill and east of the house.

The design of the walled garden is a triptych, a system Tom has experimented with elsewhere (at Cogshall Grange and Middleton Lodge). 'I thought it was interesting to divide the garden into these three very different areas,' Tom explains. 'I put this very architectural set piece [a pavilion and canal] in the middle and then made a spring garden on the west, which is very calm, with more repetition in the planting. Then on the east side I made a more intense, colourful and varied garden, with gravel paths.'

These snaking paths make their way through the planted sections of the roughly semicircular garden, creating an intimate, private feel. 'The clients felt very exposed up in the main house – they wanted somewhere secret, a little escape,' Tom explains.

Previous pages
Yellow-flowered *Asphodeline liburnica* and smokebush (*Cotinus coggygria*) dominate this part of the drier, eastern side of the garden.

Left
Siberian irises and *Amsonia tabernaemontana* var. *salicifolia*, with *Cornus kousa*, in the cooler western section.

Opposite
A grassy path wends its way towards a pavilion designed by Jamie Fobert, with *Gillenia trifoliata* (left) and *Geranium* 'Brookside' (right).

In the eastern (more 'Mediterranean') section, small trees such as multi-stemmed prunus, cotinus, cercidiphyllum and cornus help break up more or less continuous and dense rhythmic plantings of a palette of colourful perennials including perovskias, phlox, catananche, *Asphodeline liburnica*, veronicastrums, astrantias and salvias, interwoven with stachys and the grasses *Stipa brachytricha* and *Helictotrichon sempervirens*.

The western part of the garden is somewhat darker in style, with a predominantly blue, mauve and white scheme. The small tree mix is augmented by *Magnolia* x *loebneri* 'Merrill', while key subjects in the beds include *Pulmonaria* 'Blue Ensign', *Iris sibirica* 'Silver Edge' and *Gillenia trifoliata*, alongside astrantias, geraniums and *Epimedium rubrum*. Peonies erupt in summer in the southern section, while hakonechloa grass threads its way through everything.

The perimeter beds around the walled garden are more conventional in style, and shrubbier, with scores of clematis in different varieties climbing the brick walls, along with vines, roses, solanum, jasmine, elaeagnus and abelia.

The centre of the space is occupied by the long rectangle of the canal, flanked by panels of the grass *Panicum virgatum* 'Shenandoah' and informally planted *Malus* 'Evereste'. A bronze pavilion of folded appearance designed by architect Jamie Fobert, a regular collaborator of Tom's, sits at the north end of the canal. It's a dreamy, transcendent space of the kind Tom likes to insert into his garden schemes.

'When I do use water it is not just a decorative adjunct to the garden but a central element of it,' Tom says. 'Sometimes, as here, it becomes one of the organizing principles. I like the simplicity of this canal and the grass, and also the sense that you can look into something but not actually be in it – even here, at the centre of the composition. That is something we can learn from Islamic gardens: although they can be highly decorated, the fulcrum is often very simple.' The western section of the garden also features an unusual water effect: a series of fountains which have been installed for their sound alone. They automatically switch off

when someone walks by, an inversion of the usual 'water-trick' conceit, which involves spraying unwary visitors as they pass.

Up at the house, Tom re-energized the plantings around the building, using shrubs and evergreens (*Rosa* x *odorata* 'Mutabilis', nepeta, clipped box) which can cope with the large-scale environment. The terraces were added in the 1950s by the neo-Georgian architect Raymond Erith, and Tom has horticulturally enlivened each level in turn. On the top terrace are box plants in terracotta pots and on the next is a grass plat with dumpling box balls, then a rose garden (pink and white with some purples) with beds shaped like the crayfish native to the Thames. Finally there is a sculpture terrace with new stone statues of the Seasons in 18th-century, Van Nost style. A water gate at the foot of the terraces leads down a grassy slope to a landing stage on the river.

Just east of the house an existing swimming pool, with a jaunty pool-house by Erith, was formerly entirely open. Tom has enclosed it with a yew hedge planted in front with lavender, added a quartet of medlars and supplemented the scene with small box balls by the pool and olives in terracotta pots.

Southwest of the house is a remarkable rock garden, originally made in the late 19th century, which Tom renovated and extended ('it was good fun!'). He retained some gnarled old *Pinus* and *Acer* trees and added scores of alpine plants such as saxifrages, species peonies and creeping campanulas, as well as stipa grasses. Rocks were brought in to extend the feature vertically, with an extra waterfall added as well as several boulder bridges. Its clear, flowing water and fresh feel make this a highly successful addition to the garden, hidden away among dense thujas, yews and holm oaks.

Previous spread
The rose garden on the terraces below the house, with views along the River Thames and Hambleden Valley.

Left
The main terrace, adjacent to the house, with a pair of urns marking a flight of steps to the lower levels.

Opposite
The rock garden, overhung with Japanese maples.

VERGELEGEN

Previous pages
Rocks pop up across the prairie surrounding the house, designed by Tom Kundig.

Above
A dramatic drawn overview showing the property in its forested context, with the tiny paradise garden in a clearing to the right.

Opposite
Boulders moved from the surrounding landscape – here sprouting ferns and *Heuchera villosa* – have been incorporated into a path by the house.

A new house on a large estate in rural Massachusetts, by Seattle-based architect Tom Kundig, is a bold modernist take on the log-cabin aesthetic, utilizing concrete, glass and rusting steel. In Tom's view it embodies the idea of architect as 'hero' in the face of nature's grandeur. As such it is very much in the spirit of the American Sublime, embodied by the Hudson River School of painters.

The rolling wooded countryside of the Berkshires, as this area is known, was divided up in the 18th century into small fields and orchards enclosed by drystone walls. As large-scale agriculture moved westwards on to the prairies in the 19th century, the landscape was largely abandoned and recolonized by trees – so much so that today it appears almost like virgin forest.

'The house commands the landscape in this very declamatory way,' Tom comments. 'The landscape we made around it – rough terrain at the front and a not-terribly-flowery prairie – is quite intimate, so as to get away from the heroic feel of the building.'

The existing forest around the house – maple, oak and white pine – had been cleared before the arrival of Tom and his team, leaving space for a 4-hectare (10-acre) prairie of native plants using a mix formulated with the assistance of Neil Diboll, the Wisconsin nurseryman and prairie planting specialist. Tom says he found the experience of being restricted to native plants refreshing and educational: 'Almost every single plant used on this project is a native. That's the nice thing about working overseas – you don't feel the need to be "exotic". It's more interesting to confine yourself to native plantings and learn about it that way.'

VERGELEGEN 103

Left
A winding path that encircles the house is fringed with ferns and native shrubs and trees.

Opposite
The manmade swimming lake, with an old fieldstone wall beyond, left in situ.

'In the undercroft of the house we have used local ferns and sedges, as well as things like *Asarum canadense* and [the grass] *Sporobolus heterolepis*,' Tom adds. 'Then, in the open ground beyond the house we have exposed areas of rocky outcrop by using a water jet, to emphasize the wild and uncultivated quality of the place. We also collected additional rocks from the surrounding landscape and used them to accentuate an immediate roughness. We cast the concrete walk that runs around the rocks and added lots of sedges and ferns. The house had this very rhetorical, grand presence and I wanted to reintroduce a sense of balance with the landscape. Bringing a lot of rocks in seemed a good way to do that. The paving immediately around the house was made from enormous natural sheets of a local schist – some eight feet across – to maintain the monumental character.'

Behind the house and away from the epic view, there is a slightly more intimate character to the landscape. When Tom started work at the site there was a low-lying bog in this area where the previous owner had tried – and failed – to make a pond. Tom enlarged this feature to create a pool – what he calls 'a little semi-domesticated hinterland close to the house for frog-spotting, swimming and boating – but still no gardening'.

There are old-established paths running through the forest, and a beautiful river flows along the bottom edge of the property. The owners are keen equestrians, so there is stabling and fields for horses to graze. Some distance from the house, on the other side of the lake, is a collection of pre-existing cabins which are used as guest accommodation.

The only obviously cultivated 'garden' on the site is a remote and primitive enclosure, focused on a single apple tree, that is set some 365 metres (400 yards) away from the house. 'It was amazing because there was just this one rather beautiful apple tree in the middle of a glade, obviously left over from an old orchard,' Tom recalls. The tree was enclosed by a 'fence' made of rough logs

of robinia wood, and encircled with radiating beds of wild strawberries, thymes, raspberries and fan-trained peaches, cherries, gages, pears and quinces. There are also cottage-garden flowers to decorate what Tom calls his 'paradise palisade garden': heleniums, asters, amsonias, salvias, geraniums, anemones, astrantias and phlox.

'It's a play on the absurdity of the very idea of a garden,' Tom explains, 'by reducing it to its bare-minimum components. It's such a romantic idea – someone wandering through the woods and finding this garden in a stockade. The apple becomes the tree of life and the centre of this American fortified Eden. Everything inside the paradise garden is cultivated and exotic. Everything outside is a native. It's like a botanical Custer's Last Stand.'

Tom adds that the paradise garden idea also 'seemed apt for a client who was an expert on Bosch and Bruegel – both of whom made such vivid interpretations of paradise in their paintings'.

Previous pages
The view from the undercroft of the house, across a field of ferns and *Carex pensylvanica* (Pennsylvania sedge) towards the hills of the Berkshires.

Opposite
The view from the house, with amsonia giving way to solidago and echinaceas, and black walnuts beyond.

Right
A palisade of robinia wood encloses a vegetable garden of concentric beds made around an old orchard tree found on site.

COGSHALL GRANGE

Previous pages
The planting of the walled garden in its seasonal pomp, next to the central pool. The pavilion against the wall was designed by Jamie Fobert.

Above
This site drawing shows how closely the redesigned walled garden sits to the main house in this case.

Opposite
A black pine frames views out to the parkland at this small historic estate, with *Euphorbia wallichii* and echinacea in the foreground.

A classic English landscape scene greets the visitor to this country house in Cheshire. From the lime avenue lining the entrance drive there are views across serene parkland studded with old oaks and beech, and cattle and sheep grazing the fields. The four-square red-brick house of about 1840 stands in a compact and well-proportioned 40-hectare (100-acre) estate, of which approximately 3 hectares (7 acres) is considered garden, including the walled garden which stands at the heart of Tom's design. Though there is much more to this project than that.

To Tom and his clients, the house had looked a little stranded in its park, with grass flowing right up to the windows in the 'Capability' Brown manner. Tom moved the story on, opting for a more Reptonian attitude, with ornamentally gardened areas directly against the house, most intensively against its west elevation, leaving the south and east sides relatively unadorned. The north side harbours the service areas, including a stable court (now offices), a new swimming pool wing and the old walled garden.

A deconstructed version of a knot garden, set in a terrace of reclaimed York stone, occupies more than half the length of the west side of the house. Cloud-formed box hedges, resembling fat caterpillars, lend structure to soft, cottagey plantings of pink *Echinacea* 'Magnus Superior' mingling with spiky *Eryngium giganteum*, salvias, heleniums (that Tom favourite, 'Moerheim Beauty'), rudbeckias, amsonias, astrantias and (for later in the season) asters. At the corners of the beds small groups of carex and stipa grasses help buttress the perennial plantings, while masses of tulips enliven the scene in spring.

The pool-building extension gives on to its own terraced area and a small walled 'kitchen terrace', with beds planned along similar lines, but with the addition of *Rosa* x *odorata* 'Mutabilis', hellebores, Japanese anemone 'Königin Charlotte' and clematis and wisteria growing on the walls. Masses of alliums provide spring interest, while out in the western parkland are specimen trees including a Bhutanese pine, cedar of Lebanon and Monterey pine.

From here the journey through the garden continues north towards the walled garden, past quieter, moodier plantings of *Hydrangea quercifolia*, *Penstemon* 'Raven' and hellebores. This area provides a suitably muted context for the walled garden.

Passing through a gate into the walled garden, the visitor emerges into a stylized grove of ten Niwaki (cloud-pruned) hornbeams arranged roughly in two lines. Each tree has a planting bed at its base with a green and white theme: *Hosta* 'Devon Green' with *Molinia caerulea* subsp. *caerulea* 'Poul Petersen', *Epimedium rubrum* and *Rodgersia podophylla*, offset by clumps of *Selinum wallichianum*. The sculpted hornbeams and delicate white flowers set the tone for this composed and connoisseurial garden. Adjacent to the 'grove' is an arrangement of box hedges running in lines through a massed planting of more of the molinia 'Poul Petersen' – all organized according to a fingerprint pattern. Tom had wanted to use the client's fingerprint, but in the end used his own, as his client told him that this was clearly more Tom's garden than his.

'I do think about this question of "Whose garden it is anyway?",' Tom reflects. 'I think quite a lot of my effort is bound up with trying to navigate a careful line between what is didactic – making people behave in a certain way through the design – and what is not. To me, that is one of the most interesting things about making gardens. It's the tension that goes to the heart of it. And it can never be resolved.'

A canal runs parallel to the grove and 'fingerprint panel', forming the still, meditative heart of the space. Then the garden steps down a level, loosening into a much freer space set in gravel, where multiple paths wind around amorphous beds

Previous pages
The entrance to the walled garden is a stylized grove of cloud-pruned hornbeam, underplanted with *Hosta* 'Devon Green', selinum and molinia grass.

Left
The view down the pool, prefaced by the yellow daisy flowers of *Rudbeckia maxima*.

Opposite
The rudbeckia is joined by clumps of mauve *Eupatorium maculatum* 'Riesenschirm', white selinum, *Echinacea purpurea* 'Magnus' and *Calamagrostis* x *acutiflora* 'Karl Foerster'.

Previous pages
The plantings around the pool give way to massed *Molinia caerulea* subsp. *caerulea* 'Poul Petersen' grasses and then the cloud-pruned hornbeams.

Left
Rodgersia and selinum contribute to the quiet, woodland feel at the entrance of the walled garden.

planted in joyous fashion with a range of perennials – rudbeckias, baptisias, eryngiums, echinaceas, geraniums ('Mayflower') – set amid grasses including *Calamagrostis* x *acutiflora* 'Karl Foerster', *Panicum virgatum* 'Shenandoah' and *Stipa brachytricha*. Spire plants including foxgloves and *Eremurus robustus* (which throws up spires 2.5 metres/8 feet tall) add drama, while against the walls are choice shrubs, climbers and small trees including *Sophora tetraptera*, vines, trachelospermum, clematis varieties and *Schizophragma integrifolium* (Chinese hydrangea vine).

It's an immersive experience, with a circular, rhythmic feel to the paths and plantings, punctuated by small trees such as rhus, cotinus, cornus and arbutus. Tom has not used many of the bulkier, shrub-like perennials in this project, and the result is a softer, more delicate feel than plantings achieved in mainstream 'New Perennials' style.

The structure of the walled garden – divided into two distinct sections with contrasting moods, separated by the canal – was inspired by what Tom perceived as the kind of life his clients were leading. Having been successful in business, they were now looking for privacy but also enjoyment. As Tom explains: 'I made it explicit to them that the plan was inspired by the divide between the Apollonian and the Dionysian. The gravel garden represents the Dionysian – the joyful, colourful exuberant life. The other side is something else ... not strictly Apollonian, perhaps, but calmer, more ordered. The bit in the middle [the canal] is this area we tend to occupy as half-thoughtful people, where you see these two halves of life and you don't necessarily know to which you belong. I felt they were very much in that zone.'

A small pavilion by architect Jamie Fobert sits at the edge of the garden, near the canal. 'There is something important to me about this pavilion being at the edge of the garden, looking in – as if it is an observer of the action, rather than a participant in it,' Tom says. 'This is essentially an introspective garden.'

There is even more to this garden, with extensive woodland plantings and an orchard, plus a new lake and a general 'roughing up' of the areas to the north where the garden meets the landscape, to make that transition easier.

CLOSE ENCOUNTERS AND THE VIEW FROM ABOVE

—

Tom Stuart-Smith

In the fields below the house where I was born, and just a few hundred yards from where I still live, there is a dell, a medieval chalk pit. In the early 19th century when the house was given a Regency makeover the dell was planted up with beech trees to make a picturesque clump. Every year in spring I walk down through the fields, climb to the top of one of the beech trees on the edge of the dell and sit there for a while.

There must be dozens of different ways to climb the tree and the way down is never the same as the way up. Perhaps my favourite way of getting into it is to pull one of the lower branches down to the ground and simply walk on to it as if on to a springy gangplank. I can then reach up and grasp the branch above the one I am standing on and use this to keep my balance as I walk along the lower branch towards the trunk. As I creep gingerly forward, the branches gradually lift me off the ground till I am about ten feet up at the point where the branch joins the trunk. The canopy closes around me; levitation and immersion combined. I like climbing in spring more than any other time because the green of the young leaves is so edibly fresh and I can see more: the sinuous form of the whole tree, the surrounding fields and sky visible through a gauze of leaf and branch. Later in summer, the ascent becomes more intimate, climbing under a veil of dense green.

I can reach right to the top of the tree so my head pokes above the branches about 70 feet up. Sometimes birds fly quite close and even land nearby in the tree; often I can watch the cows in the field going about their business. I can see up the slope towards the house and the walled garden, and down the valley where the woods crowd in on either side. There is a delicious sense of disappearing into the background and feeling, for an illusory moment, a part of it all. In one sense I go to the tree in order to escape, and yet the experience is also about trying to connect – of learning more thoroughly how the ground lies and how the place is put together. I have come to think that many of my gardening and designing efforts are to some extent an attempt to recreate the experience of being in the tree. The mix of freedom and embrace, of living in the moment and being an analyst of the scene.

Gardening does not give us such a direct experience of nature as being in the tree, but it does enable us to explore countless different ways of relating to the natural world. With me it began much more prosaically, as a way of keeping my teenage self occupied outside the house. My parents encouraged this and allowed me frighteningly free rein. Soon I was planting trees, visiting gardens and buying plants, and of course making plans for the transformation of our pocket Eden. Looking at an early list in my notebook from 1978 I find an order from Hillier Nurseries. It includes the following: *Acer cappadocicum* 'Aureum' (Ouch!), *Cedrus atlantica* 'Glauca' (where did I think I was going to put that?), *Lamium maculatum* 'Chequers' (horrid little thing; largely obliterated from memory), *Juniperus* 'Grey Owl' (what was I thinking?) and *Daboecia cantabrica* f. *alba* (a sweet little heathy shrub, but completely unsuited to dry, gravelly Hertfordshire). In some of these cases I would have seen a plant at Westonbirt or Kew perhaps and thought it attractive. In other cases the *Hillier Manual* or W. J. Bean's great five-part tome may have been to blame. These were my bedtime reading, and yes, I see the *Daboecia* described as 'one of the most charming of small shrubs' and the juniper as being a 'splendid plant'.

It now seems a scatter-gun collection with little logic beyond that of intense curiosity and a certain acquisitiveness. In most cases it is fortunate that not many of these early plantings survived. Sometimes this is because I realized what dreadful things I had done and duly undid them while no one was watching. On other occasions I couldn't get away with this. I find another entry in the notebook for 1979 for 54 beech plants and suddenly remember that this was to replace a hedge of Leyland cypress I planted as one of my first forays into the garden aged about seventeen. I soon appreciated what a terrible thing I'd done and asked to be allowed to take it out and replace it with beech. My father said I could, as long as I replanted the cypresses somewhere else. I duly found homes for them all in the most out of the way places and spent the next ten years furtively poisoning or ring-barking them. Now there are still half a dozen dotted around the landscape; they are about 80 feet tall and just getting into their stride.

So my first efforts were not natural in any way at all. It was all red-hot pokers, Leyland cypress and junipers. I was in thrall to novelty.

Hadspen, Sissinghurst, Hidcote and Kiftsgate. These were the early gardens I visited and admired in my late teens. Grand drawing-room sort of gardens, mostly planted by women who really understood about how to grow plants and how to craft a delicate sense of laissez-faire. The most convincing planting was set within a frame of formality, with the groups of plants organized into tidy clumps that burgeoned and flopped just to the point of acceptable disorder before being smartly cut back in autumn. Of all these gardens I think it was Sissinghurst that had the greatest impact. I was enraptured by the corridors and interconnecting spaces of this great garden, but above all it was the experience of climbing the tower that I recall. From here, everything was made clear. After being lost in this magical garden for hours, then to be able to see where I had been and understand how it all interconnected and related to the fields, ponds and woods around was a revelation; it was an almost out-of-body experience to see where I had been so recently and from such a different perspective. The memory of the view has forever transformed the experience of being in the view.

For my twenty-first birthday I went with my girlfriend to visit gardens in Cornwall and Devon. The scale of it all was breathtaking. I vividly remember Caerhays, with magnolias 80 feet tall flowering overhead and again on a distant hillside so that the entire landscape seemed lifted from another world; and Knightshayes, where the hellebores and scillas intermingled in great generous drifts under corylopsis. Two glimpses of an impossible heaven; gardens released from the comparative straitjacket of formal enclosures and borders.

After three years at Cambridge drawing the skulls of extinct reptiles and discovering I wasn't cut out to be a scientist I went to Manchester University to study for a degree in landscape design. For much of my time there my enthusiasm for planting the world appeared irrelevant to a career which seemed to be much more about how to drain a car park. But a considerable bright spot came in the form of our tutor Alan Ruff, a passionate urban ecologist. In the first year he took us to a beautiful and rather abandoned plot of ground near his home in New Mills, on the edge of the Peak District, where for the previous twenty years birch and alder scrub had been re-colonizing a hillside. He told us to choose a section of this vegetation and make a map of it, square metre by square metre, noting the height and the spread of every plant, creating the drawing in several layers to show the canopy, the under-storey and the ground layer. It was a crucially instructive lesson in what a natural distribution of plants is like and how this pattern looks when translated to paper – the codification of naturalism.

Alan took us on a field trip to the Netherlands. We spent a week visiting the extraordinary heemparks (habitat parks), including one of the first, the Thijssepark in Amstelveen, near Amsterdam, which

A photograph of the Thijssepark, Amstelveen, taken by Tom in 1984.

had been planted in the 1940s. This is a 2-kilometre long sliver of land about 70 metres wide designed by Christiaan P. Broerse and maintained by the municipality. It is planted with native species and made with the explicit intention of capturing some of the quality of the disappearing Dutch landscape and flora. I came away wondering why I would ever want to use an exotic plant in a garden? The hand of design was so subtle as to be almost invisible and nearly all the effect was achieved by variations of form, texture and enclosure. Since then I have always thought primarily in terms of spatial effect, character, atmosphere, texture and form, before worrying about colour.

I worked for a couple of years on my own from 1986, when my wife Sue and I first moved to The Barn at Serge Hill in Hertfordshire, where we still are and where we started to make a small garden. During this period, one very valuable experience came through Penelope Hobhouse, who was a friend of my parents. This was working on the garden of a beautiful Lutyens house called Plumpton Place.

I had visited Penny first at Hadspen and then at Tintinhull and marvelled at her mastery of colour, the stately elegance of the planting, with just a hint of déshabillé. When Penny was at Tintinhull with her husband John Malins she was at first constantly frustrated by the National Trust, who wanted everything in the garden to remain in aspic, as they perceived the creator, Mrs Reiss, had left it some twenty years before. Penny had met Mrs Reiss once or twice for tea just as she was getting the gardening bug in her time at Hadspen. So now when the National Trust suggested that some particularly dowdy planting should be 'restored', she resorted to subterfuge and announced that 'when I discussed the planting of this part of the garden with Mrs Reiss, in some depth, she said it would be much better if we took it all out and started again'. Of course, Mrs Reiss had never said anything of the sort, but the Trust knew they couldn't compete. I showed Penny my early planting plans for Plumpton, in which I was using just about every plant I knew. 'I think a little bit of repetition would be an idea' was the response. So, often, when I am giving advice to someone on planting, Penny's words ring in my ears: pare it down and repeat.

As part of the Plumpton project I met the great plantsman Jim Russell. I didn't quite appreciate at first what a very grand figure he was in the horticultural firmament, but I had seen the Rose Garden at Castle Howard in its prime, and either Penny or I suggested to my client that Jim might design a rose garden at Plumpton. Jim was a model of generosity and a very remarkable designer of planting. He kindly invited Sue and me and our baby daughter Rose to Castle Howard, where he seemed to have a free rein to do what he liked in the garden for his old Etonian friend George Howard. Our walk through Ray Wood in that June of 1987 was a revelation for me. White hesperis was naturalized through open glades, roses cascaded out of trees and scented species rhododendrons perfumed the air. I remember seeing three different forms of *Rosa soulieana* growing quite close to one other – one a great mass of a shrub over 12 feet across, another quite a small and dense thing creeping along the ground and the third the seedling named 'Wickwar', arching 30 feet out of a tree. It was the first time that I realized that giving something a species name could often be just the beginning of the story. There was an effortless grace to the composition and so much was achieved by using a few plants to knit everything together, which then made it possible to include smaller botanical distractions.

From 1988 I temporarily abandoned the idea of working for myself. It was too lonely and I didn't want to get stuck down a cul de sac of working on private gardens. But I was beginning to expand the garden at home. Initially this was just a strip around the house, but by 1991 we were able to buy some more land and started colonizing the void which had been empty acres of wheat. This involved a lot of physical hard work and the occasional ascent into the lime trees in my mother's garden next door, from where I could look down and see what sort of slow progress I was making. It was still early days. I didn't have the space, knowledge or cash to break out into large naturalistic plantings, which seemed to be confined to the territory of the great aristocratic woodland gardens. That aesthetic had not yet popped out of the rhododendron thicket on to the lawn.

I worked very happily for Elizabeth Banks through the 1990s. I continued to learn a good deal about plants, but it all tended to be within a tight frame. We were designing rather traditionally structured gardens, with formal hedged enclosures and borders with big plants at the back and little ones at the front. My steepest learning curve came when I was asked to design some planting at Rosemoor for the RHS and was occasionally supervised by Chris Brickell, one of the most knowledgeable plantsmen I have ever met and the kindest of tutors.

It was the encounter with Piet Oudolf's work which encouraged me, along with so many others, to plant on a more expansive scale. I had read about some of the Dutch and German work with perennials but had never visited Westpark in Munich or Piet's nursery at Hummelo in the Netherlands. But Piet's garden for John Coke at Bury Court was eye-opening. I recall seeing the meadow of *Deschampsia cespitosa* with *Trifolium rubens* scattered through it like loose purple confetti. By today's standards the garden layout seems quite mannered, but there was the beginning of a freeing-up of the plan so that plants were not just arranged in linear sequences but were all around, interacting in countless, often unforeseen ways. The balance between man and plant was readdressed in favour of the plant. This seems to me the important catalyst. Using plants in these larger expanses inevitably means getting away from composing a merely linear flower arrangement, where plants seem like lines of suspects subjected to the scrutiny of an ID parade. The viewer is forced to ask, how do these plants relate

Hummelo, on a trip made by the Tom Stuart-Smith design studio to the Netherlands.

Tom and daughter Rose at The Barn in Hertfordshire, planting the first yew hedges in 1989.

to one another? It's then a short step to looking into how they grow in their natural habitat.

I saw the Bury Court meadow, which is actually quite a modest area, in its prime, before the *Deschampsia* died out and the clover went rather leggy. It had such simple grace, as if it were just getting on with its own business of being grass and clover. Growing, flowering, and of course dying. Piet is the evangelist of decay.

At this time I was filling my own garden with short-lived verbascums, giant thistles and other unruly things that suckered, seeded and generally misbehaved. It was up to me to keep them in check. This is all very well on your own watch or if you are lucky enough to work with a gardener with lots of patience and understanding, but I gradually learnt that the spontaneous and slightly disorderly look I was drawn to had to be reined in a little if it (and me, I suppose) wasn't to come off the rails. I remember once coming quite spectacularly unstuck when I enthusiastically recommended a clump of *Sambucus ebulus*, the handsome herbaceous dwarf elder, for a planting on heavy clay in the middle of France. The elder duly helped itself and in nine months covered an area about half the size of a tennis court, engulfing all before it in an inexorable flow of green. Sometimes a plant can be just a bit too happy.

As I developed my own practice I was able to expand my garden at home and my experimentations with plants accelerated. The garden began to take some shape and various patterns started to fall into place about how I was using plants.

I moved away from the idea of having very different types of planting in different areas of the garden, which I think I had inherited from all those Arts and Crafts gardens I had visited. This seemed more a collector's approach than one in which planting is a tool to create and manipulate the atmosphere of a place. Instead I gravitated towards the concept that planting is like a medium that can flow between spaces, gradually being transformed by them to take on a character that emphasizes the physical setting or the desired mood in relation to the nature of the surroundings. So there might be a subtle gradient of change between different parts of a garden, but not sudden discontinuities.

The main gradient tends to be from a more cultivated character close to the house, where I might include half-hardy plants like the occasional dahlia, penstemon and salvia, to a wilder approach on the periphery, where such plants would feel out of place. Here on the boundaries it's foxgloves, cenolophium, cranesbills – all plants that look as if they belong in a hedgerow and seem almost like some native scene, but slightly different also.

Somewhat related to this is the idea of momentum in a garden. This might be a diagonal movement across a space that runs against the formal structure of a garden, as at Mount St John, where various clipped plants – be they beech or box or *Crataegus × lavalleei* – form a strong patterning across the garden, or at Culham Court, where low box moves through the space, suggesting a formalized version of colonization, for example in the way gorse appears to pour down a hillside with an almost liquid quality. This creates the sense that the plants are organized according to their own rules, regardless of our intentions.

Sometimes this repetition of more structured planting or topiary forms a strong counterpoint to other patterning. I am particularly drawn to using simple topiary shapes that either have some kind of human proportion or a more straightforward outline reminiscent of a tree. The topiary then has an ambiguity about it, occupying a half-way state between the natural and artificial and performing a role in the garden somewhat akin to that of figurative sculpture.

In other gardens where I am not wanting to emphasize a particular directional movement I would by contrast use more of an even tapestry pattern, so that there is a sense of being in a balanced, non-directional space with a more composed and static quality of repose – as for example in a small oak and hazel coppice where there may not be great variations in flora from one end to another, so that it has a feeling of evenness and completeness. An example of this is the spring garden in the walled garden at Culham Court, where the planting is composed of regularly repeated groups and drifts, rather like a patchwork quilt made of perhaps a dozen different fabrics: amsonias, *Iris sibirica*, peonies, cranesbills and so on.

I find it helpful to think of planting in terms of comparison to an archetype. For example, the planting in the spring garden at Culham is loosely based on the scale of a hazel coppice, with trees such as multi-stemmed cornus, malus and prunus substituting for hazels, but giving that same familiar sense of scale. Some plants, by approximating closely in colour, texture or habit to well-known wild flowers also lend a sense of partial familiarity to a designed planting, which I think gives a kind of tug on the subconscious and adds a greater depth of appreciation. This might explain the attraction of umbellifers such as cenolophium or ammi, which if used in the right way remind us of native cow parsley or Queen Anne's Lace. Similarly, using a fair proportion of grasses in planting is an obvious idea if the intention is to connect the concept of the cultivated garden to more natural vegetation.

But however hung up you might be on archetypes and other design notions, there is absolutely no substitute for hard knowledge – and just occasionally, there are pioneers who really make a difference. In the past fifteen years two such inspirations for me have been Cassian Schmidt and James Hitchmough.

I first visited Cassian at the Hermannshof garden in Weinheim near Frankfurt in about 2006, with Piet Oudolf. I particularly wanted to look at the new prairie plantings he had made on different soils in the garden. Many of the plants he was using he had collected on a number of trips to parts of the US where the climate and conditions reflected those in central Germany. He then looked in detail at the ecological requirements of each species and how they relate to other species when growing in the wild, and came up with a number of matrices in which plants of similar competitive ability could be grown together on soil adjusted to those requirements. The matrix would then be repeated so it might cover an area the size of a small car park.

Each matrix is made up of about 40 per cent grasses and 60 per cent perennials (or forbs, if you are really going to speak the language). Different plants fill different niches within the mix. One area of ground had lava stone added to make it especially impoverished, and all the plants used are adapted to these poor, dry conditions. Low, clumpy tufts of prairie dropseed grass (*Sporobolus heterolepis*) are combined with light and airy *Echinacea pallida* and dark rust-red *Ratibida columnifera*. Clumps of *Symphyotrichum oblongifolium* and *Penstemon digitalis* occupy the middle ground, as does *Monarda bradburiana*, a completely bulletproof, mildew-resistant bergamot species. Many plants are, in themselves, not especially spectacular, but form the stuffing and texture of the matrix, which comprises up to fifteen different species. The overall effect of these repeated matrices is an apparently effortless, sweeping and colourful naturalism.

On the far side of the garden a contrasting area of planting is based on the European equivalent of the prairie, with sedums, achilleas, stipas, salvias and so on. A wonderful sight in June maybe, but at the end of September it is a graveyard of brown stem and dried husk. The contrast with the North American prairie – which is still green and flowering well into autumn – could not be more marked. The key to this contrast lies

Prairie planting at Hermannshoff, Germany.

in the ecology. The prairies were managed for tens of thousands of years by the Native American peoples by means of regular burning, in order to herd the bison and prevent the growth of trees. To survive this summer heat and the freezing winters, most prairie plants have deep tap roots and tend to be fairly late into growth, with correspondingly late flowering.

To me what is most enthralling about the planting at the Hermannshof garden is the paradox that out of a formulaic grid, and rather geeky detail, comes such beauty. The 10 by 10 grid of Latin names is a kind of poetic distillation. It can be seen rather like the genetic code, the intrinsic nature of the planting, which then, subject to the vagaries of nurture, is transformed into something of enormous subtlety. A fabric that fades here and shines there, that is constantly changing and is managed rather than gardened. Planting becomes more about enabling and observing a process than about fixing a picture.

This concept of planting as some magic matrix inexorably leads towards the potential of working with seedlings rather than nursery-grown plants. With this approach, there might be 100 plants per square metre rather than 10, with perhaps 15 different species in that square metre. It makes possible a level of complexity that is normally associated with a wildflower meadow, but potentially using exotic plants. This leads me to the brilliant work of James Hitchmough, who pioneered this technique and with whom I have collaborated over a period of more than fourteen years – my closest encounter being in my own garden.

In 2010 I sprayed half an acre of grass and covered the ground with 7.5 centimetres (3 inches) of sharp sand to suppress the native weed seed and provide a good free-draining seed bed. I then sowed directly into the sand an eye-wateringly expensive packet of seed selected by James: echinaceas from the American prairies, hesperantha from the South African Cape, dianthus from the Mediterranean, penstemons from Mexico. In the first year we had to water the prairie regularly so that the sand didn't dry out while the seed was germinating, and by June a remarkably even distribution of unfamiliar seedlings started to pop up. It wasn't straightforward, though. The weeding was easy enough, but there was a huge amount of it. I also hadn't reckoned on the healthy population of worms that was in the soil before we started work, and they didn't especially appreciate being part of a large aesthetic experiment and being covered in a thick layer of sand. So they spent the next year happily pulling the old soil up through the sand and depositing their little casts on the top, whereupon buttercup seed in the soil germinated by the million.

Now in autumn the prairie is at its most colourful. There are perhaps twenty different species in flower and the effect is astonishing. Starting at the top is a bunch of yellow daisy flowers led by the 3-metre (10-ft) tall compass plant (*Silphium laciniatum*). This is something straight out of Maurice Sendak; from a rosette of jagged leaves, like an acanthus on speed, rises a prodigious totem of a flower spike that waves around in a wind, counterpoised by a determined 3-metre long tap root at the other end.

At a lower level there are about forty different species battling it out, from the European Carthusian pink (*Dianthus carthusianorum*) in early summer, various penstemons from Mexico, galtonias, *Berkheya* and hesperantha from South Africa, eryngiums, assorted rudbeckias, asters, liatris and delicate little white-flowered *Euphorbia corollata* from the American prairies. It's a pan-global, botanical bun fight. Wave after wave of flower washes over the garden from late June to October and the first frosts.

And amazingly, there are almost no weeds. They don't much like the idea of germinating in the sand and the soil is quite poor anyway, so if they do germinate it's not too difficult to stop them becoming established. A given area takes about 10 per cent of the time to look after, compared with the main garden.

The poverty of the soil is really important in all this. If it was too rich, the more aggressive species would be impossible to control and the whole thing would soon become a boring mass of just two or three species. As it is, the most time-consuming exercise is pulling out asters, which tend to multiply gradually, at the expense of everything else.

I remember 2013, the first season that my home prairie really got into its stride. I used to walk around it in a daze. Part of this was simply the joy of the spectacle and the astonishing novelty of it all – such unfamiliar plants all jostling together. It made me appreciate the importance of surprise and complexity in planting, in that it makes you look three times more closely at the detail. But more than anything else, it is the experience of total immersion that I love. I am enveloped in it completely, it is all around me. In contrast to the rest of the garden, where things are framed, shaped and carefully curated, it is a wonderfully unmediated and considerably less civilized experience.

One of my favourite views of the prairie is to stand back from this close encounter, to withdraw from the fine detail of this plant next to that, and to climb up an old oak tree beyond the eastern edge, where, from my perch, the crazy complexity recedes so that it becomes part of the bigger garden composition; a brightly lit patch stitched into a garden of patches, and then into a landscape of larger patches. From here in the tree, it is almost as if my mind's eye is holding a soft pencil ready to sketch and analyse the scene, to see how one part relates to another and how the whole relates to the wider setting of fields and lanes and hedges. My foothold half way up the tree seems almost to represent my life as a designer.

Coming down from the tree, I shed the analytical self and am soon in the midst of it all again. In September as I write this, the silphiums and coreopsis are still in flower above my head, with the foliage of the latter turning a deep red that picks up the dark plum of New England asters. Black-eyed Susans and smaller asters form a lower wash of colour, and occasional clumps of the big bluestem prairie grass rise through this to a height of almost nine feet. The goldfinches are feeding in flocks on the seedheads and I am in it up to my neck.

The prairie in The Barn garden as seen from the vantage point of an old oak tree.

Tradition

WINDSOR CASTLE

WYCLIFFE HALL

MADRESFIELD COURT

YOTES COURT

FORT BELVEDERE

WINDSOR CASTLE

WINDSOR CASTLE

Previous pages
Integral to Tom's plan was the idea of 'embowering' the castle once more in its parkland setting, by means of greensward and larger trees such as *Catalpa bignonioides* (centre), tulip tree (left) and lime (right).

Above
An early coloured sketch of the design for the route up to the castle, with the shrubbery garden to the right. In the event the path was significantly widened.

Opposite
Big-scale shrub borders are appropriate to the castle setting, with the addition of sturdy perennials such as purple *Geranium* 'Brookside'.

As the 'client' for this project was ultimately HM The Queen, the stakes were already raised high enough. In addition, the site held considerable emotional resonance for Tom, as he had spent five years when a boy as a chorister in St George's Chapel, inside the castle precincts, and therefore grew up with an intimate knowledge of how the castle, town and Windsor Great Park interact.

The brief was to create a garden to celebrate the Queen's Diamond Jubilee in 2012. Tom's vision was to design a garden setting that would enhance the experience of the thousands of daily visitors who walk up to the castle entrance (at the Edward III Tower) from the ticket office. Formerly, this area was a car park with a wide road running through it. Tom succeeded in narrowing the roadway and having the car park moved, though the loss of parking facilities 'on the doorstep' ultimately proved too controversial for some of those who live and work at the castle, so the design had to be adjusted. A smaller car park is now hidden behind trees and shrubs on the south side.

'The idea was to see this garden as an extension of the Sandby picturesque,' Tom explains, referring to the 18th-century artist Thomas Sandby, who completed a number of celebrated paintings which evocatively recorded the castle in its setting, and who was responsible for the Picturesque transformation of Windsor.

As Tom describes it, 'The long-term vision is to see this as part of a landscape of avenues at Windsor, and across it all this wash of park-like Picturesque. I feel the main achievement was to get some big trees planted close to the castle – we have put in more holm oak and lime, particularly – though some of them have been taken

out subsequently because of light problems in the castle's private apartments.' He continues, 'It's also a great pity that the drive was widened from the size I had originally envisaged: it would have been charming and low-key, but now it feels like a B-road that goes straight up through the castle. This is about the only job that I make apologies for, though I do think it is a success in some ways, especially if you know what it was like before, when it was pretty terrible – just a huge car park.'

On the right (south) side of the route up to the castle is the most intense area of planting in the scheme, comprised of an alternative walkway for visitors which takes them along a winding path shaded by multi-stemmed holm oaks, *Cornus kousa*, *Magnolia* x *loebneri* 'Leonard Messel' and a tulip tree (*Liriodendron tulipifera*).

Tucked into a recess in this shrubbery is a large, raised York stone plinth, 10 metres (33 feet) across, which functions as a bandstand during the summer months. Contrasting Purbeck limestone and Cumbrian slate have been inlaid to form a 16-pointed star. At the centre of this is a further star: a bronze medal, 1 metre (3 feet) wide, of the Order of the Garter, the most senior order of knighthood to be conferred by the sovereign. The historical 'headquarters' of the Order, which was founded in 1348 by Edward III, is St George's Chapel, situated just a few hundred yards from the garden.

The planting is slightly darker and shrubbier at the beginning (western end) of the walkway, with philadelphus, viburnum, osmanthus, sarcococca, box, roses, hydrangeas and euphorbias, before lightening somewhat on the other side of the bandstand, with herbaceous plants including foxgloves, campanulas, phlomis, peonies and ferns contributing a fresher, flowery appeal.

On the other (north) side of the visitor route to the castle, Tom has softened the appearance of the castle walls around the Saxon Tower with small trees such as the strawberry tree, *Arbutus unedo*, and wall plantings of *Magnolia grandiflora*, lilac, clematis, wisteria and roses (such as 'Seagull', 'Rambling Rector', 'Nyveldt's White'

Previous pages
A path winds through the shrubbery that is hidden to one side of the main walkway up to the castle, with purple *Campanula lactiflora* and *Cornus kousa* in flower above.

Left
A glimpse of the 'embowered' castle.

Opposite
Euphorbia, nepeta and cranesbill geraniums complement views to the mottled grey castle walls.

Opposite
The quieter, lower section of the shrubbery walk, with a glimpse of fragrant *Rosa rugosa* 'Roseraie de l'Hay'.

Right
The view towards the royal family's private apartments. It is easy to forget that the whole of Windsor town and castle are so close to the Royal Park, and Tom's intention was to 'bring the park to the town'.

and 'Blanc Double de Coubert'). Around them are ground-covering groups of *Geranium* 'Brookside' with *Persicaria amplexicaulis* 'Rosea', *Helianthus salicifolius*, *Centranthus ruber* 'Albus' and *Hydrangea paniculata* 'Kyushu'. The suitably regal dark tulip 'Queen of Night' pops up in spring.

Another aspect of Tom's work at Windsor Castle was the replanting of the Moat Garden, a dramatically sunken space at the foot of the Round Tower, which castle visitors can peer down into but not enter. 'It was a very curious garden when we arrived,' Tom recalls, 'a collection of bits and pieces, all rather private and amateurish. We looked at what was first done there in the late 19th century, which was very much in the cottage-garden style, and felt we didn't want to change that rather sweet feel.' The planting here has been refreshed with dramatic plants such as cardoons, *Melianthus major* and verbascum, complemented by the likes of fennel, erigeron, campanula and *Salvia* 'Amistad'.

'I always saw the garden at Windsor Castle as an extension of the Picturesque landscape of the town,' Tom says by way of summary. 'Previously it all felt very remote. The garden has now succeeded in bringing the treed landscape of the Great Park right down into the centre of Windsor.'

WYCLIFFE HALL

WYCLIFFE HALL

Previous pages
The view from the terrace walk across the walled garden, with the cliffs overhanging the River Tees visible in the distance.

Above
The proposed formal garden against the Georgian house's facade is shown in this design drawing, which also celebrates the giant cedar, at left.

Opposite
Clipped yew cones and bracketed hedges define the garden laid out in front of the house.

For the unprepared visitor, the isolated rural setting of Wycliffe Hall, near Barnard Castle in Co. Durham, might seem almost forgettable: a small park studded with specimen trees prefacing a four-square mid-Georgian house (1760) of buff Teesdale stone. There is a fine old cedar in the middle of the turning circle to one side of the house, and a jaunty clipped yew 'elephant' hedge beyond that, but otherwise apparently little else to distinguish it from other attractive small estates in the region.

It is only when the visitor ventures behind the house that the true medieval savour of the place becomes apparent, as well as the stupendous views over the River Tees and the cliffs which rise above it along this stretch – giving rise to the name of the property, Wycliffe, or 'white cliff'. The spot was a magnet for 'Picturesque tourists' of the late 18th and early 19th century, with J.M.W. Turner visiting to paint a scene which is now in the collection of the Tate. It transpires that this is an ancient pele tower, a small fortified house which was later 'Georgianized' by a new owner (rejoicing in the name of Marmaduke Tunstall) in fashionable style, with big sash windows and ashlar facings.

Tom's plan for the (south) entrance front was to create a formal garden directly beneath the facade of the house, which would be perfectly in scale. A regular series of yew compartments enclose deep borders of perennial plants and grasses in rich green and purple tones, facing each other across the central sward. The dark colour palette suits the architectural formality and the mottled grey stone, while parallel lines of clipped yew cones accentuate the axis and create a link with the small park beyond, where Tom has added oaks and chestnuts to what was originally a rather

Previous pages
Soft pink *Thalictrum aquilegifolium*, *Iris sibirica* 'Silver Edge' and purple astrantias in the border, with the dovecote beyond.

Left
A ha-ha divides the small park from the garden by the house, which was remodelled in Palladian style in 1760.

Opposite
The 'Elizabethan' garden behind the house, with lead balls on oak posts, bay trees in boxes and the curving edge of Ptolemy Dean's bastion terrace visible in the background.

bare space. The yew cones are also in scale with a charming dovecote possessed of a fortified air.

Tom admits that what has been achieved here is not at all in the 18th-century manner, which would have required sward right up to the house, or else (in Reptonian mode) some modest plantings under the windows. 'It's more what the Victorians would have done,' he says. 'But I took the view that the park was small and people have to live here. You need to provide a sense of welcome – and this is like a "party front". Of course, the owners could live in the kitchen garden around the back, but why should they?'

The first inkling the visitor has of the riverine setting is a view from a belvedere at one end of the terrace under the south-facing facade, down into a tangled ravine with a tributary of the River Tees hidden far below (but delightfully audible). This belvedere was designed by architect Ptolemy Dean, and was the first significant collaboration with Tom.

The preferred garden route from here is not directly around the back of the house, but via a route which takes the visitor over beyond the 'elephant' hedge, where there is a new orchard. This is bounded by a wall with a terrace walk on top, lined with narrow columnar Irish yews, and with a long west-facing border along its 85-metre (280-ft) length. This border is rhythmically planted with grasses such as *Miscanthus sinensis* 'Malepartus' and 'Gracillimus', and perennial plantings based around *Veronicastrum virginicum* 'Fascination', *Perovskia* 'Blue Spire', *Eupatorium rugosum* 'Chocolate', *Euphorbia palustris* and eremurus. Smaller subjects include *Astrantia major* 'Claret', *Limonium platyphyllum* 'Violetta', amsonia, phlox, achillea and knautia.

The terrace deposits the visitor on the valley's edge, with a first breathtaking view of the shallow but fast-flowing river as it stretches away (this is good fly-fishing country). Behind the house is a cramped but characterful ensemble of spaces

redolent of the medieval history of the house, intensified by Tom by means of a small parterre of evergreen hedge enclosures with painted wooden posts topped by orbs, in Tudor style. Steps lead up to a bastion viewpoint, lent character by a single hawthorn tree.

The walled vegetable garden lies next to the orchard, beyond a swimming pool with lawn flanked by elegant new glasshouses (designed by Dean). This is no fancy formal potager but is much more 'medieval' in feel, on this sloping, unevenly shaped space. Box-lined, brick-edged beds are criss-crossed by paths of grey-brown gravel, and pear and apple trees are intermixed, giving it almost the air of a smallholding. A peony walk with metal arch supports adds a dose of country-house glamour. Close attention was paid to elements such as gates, fences and walls, which were in many cases replaced to create a sense of estate unity. The most dramatic addition in this regard was a new set of front gates, based on those designed by Isaac Ware for the Admiralty in the mid-18th century.

'What I wanted to do here was accentuate the Janus-like quality of the place,' Tom says. 'So I made the 18th-century front into a beautifully laid-out drawing room, which you see from the entrance drive as this charming little set-piece. It makes the contrast so much stronger – between all the horticulture at the front, and the drama of the cliffs and river valley behind the house.'

Previous pages
The raised terrace walk, with the orchard to one side and a line of fastigiate Irish yews on the other. The planting in this part of the border at this season is dominated by yellow *Telekia speciosa*.

Opposite
The River Tees and the cliffs in all their glory. The bank down to the water's edge has been turned into meadow.

Right
The sloping walled garden adds to the pleasingly antiquated feel of the place, while recent architectural additions (a conservatory and glasshouse) are sympathetic to the house and its setting.

MADRESFIELD COURT

MADRESFIELD COURT

Previous pages
A 'jewel-box' garden was commissioned for this compact space set within the moated environs of a fabled English house, its interior richly decorated in the late 19th century.

Above
The jewel-like quality of Tom's new garden next to the house can be appreciated in this design drawing. The garden is enclosed by the moat, with the existing formal gardens beyond, medieval stew (fish) ponds at left and woodland encroaching almost up to the house walls.

Opposite
The view through a casement window to the garden and the central decorative well head surrounded by fleurs-de-lys box hedges.

To a great Tudor house (with important Victorian additions) which has been in the same family for more than 900 years, Tom has contributed a sophisticated, jewel-like garden, simple in its form but possessed of many facets and reflecting different historical periods. Madresfield Court, in Worcestershire, is mainly celebrated today for its highly decorative late 19th-century, Arts and Crafts interiors, notably the library by C.R. Ashbee and Henry Payne's chapel. This context provided the inspiration for the garden – and how could it not?

'I was very struck by the chapel,' Tom explains. 'It is this very interesting mix between the Victorian High Church aesthetic and the fact that this house is to some extent a "play house". I thought the garden should reflect that – it should have an element of historicist seriousness, but should also be something quite playful and decorated. Because the house is so much about decoration. Ultimately I felt the garden had to have a similarly dense grain to the house – this wasn't the place to come up with a modernist expression.'

The garden is an approximate rectangle focused on an existing stone well head with a decorative ironwork canopy. Its stepped surround takes the form of a Tudor rose – as does the area of lawn surrounding it – with urns and suitably 'medieval' plantings of rosemary, lavender and thyme. The well head is set within this central panel of grass, with four fleur-de-lys-shaped, box-hedged beds at the corners, each containing roses ('Munstead Wood', 'Gruss an Aachen' and 'Wild Edric'), which are underplanted with a mix of alliums, helianthemums, eryngiums, verbascums and nepeta.

The fleur-de-lys theme was in part inspired by the Ladies' Garden at Broughton Castle, Oxfordshire, another supremely romantic moated garden, which was in that case laid out in the 1880s – at the same time as Madresfield was being transformed from Tudor manor house to High Victorian fantasy. Tom was alive to the fact that the two places have a distant connection via the Beauchamp Earls of Warwick in the 14th century. If this historical context sounds a little *recherché*, it is perhaps as well to remember that the generation of the family growing up in the house now is the thirtieth to have lived at Madresfield.

The essential formality of the space is emphasized by a series of pencil-thin yew topiaries, reminiscent of the pinnacles on a medieval cathedral – a suitably Gothic reference. 'Eventually I want the yew topiaries to be about 4 metres (13 feet) high and a maximum of 80 centimetres (30 inches) wide at the base – as thin as a bodkin,' Tom comments. 'They should look like the trees you see in medieval illuminated manuscripts.'

The architectural feel of the garden's structure plays off the detail and complexity of the house facade, with its decorative brickwork, elaborate stone dressings and ornamentations, with multiple gables, friezes, chimneys and windows in various forms.

The profuse planting within this structure is as rich, dense and sumptuous as a Renaissance brocade, with phlox, geraniums, salvias, dianthus, helianthemums and yet more roses cascading into each other, but given some room and space by the addition of certain grasses and larger perennials, such as *Molinia caerulea* subsp. *arundinacea* 'Transparent', along with stipas, panicums and perovskia. There are larger shrubs and climbers near and against the house on the north and west side, such as *Hydrangea quercifolia*, *Euphorbia* x *pasteurii* and old-fashioned roses including 'Moonlight', 'Cornelia' and 'Veilchenblau'.

A large paved terrace with dining table has been added to the northern end of the space, for this is a family garden, while at the southern end, by the chapel,

Left
The moat, garden walls (with clumps of romneya) and chapel create an incomparable setting for intensive, decorative horticulture.

Opposite
A quieter moment: *Hydrangea quercifolia* and dark-leaved *Euphorbia* x *pasteurii* gather above *Geranium* 'Patricia'.

Previous pages
The garden is an immersive experience – here, yellow *Asphodeline liburnica* is flowering with white rose 'Kew Gardens', flanked by *Stipa gigantea*, with cistus in the foreground.

Opposite
Dawn in the garden, with the purple tones of *Salvia nemorosa* 'Amethyst' singing out, and the misty park beyond.

Right
The box fleur-de-lys hedges contain plantings of roses as a formal complement to the well head.

is a smaller octagonal sun-trap terrace surrounded on all sides by a gravelly garden of more Mediterranean feel. Here, a network of informal pathways wanders around plantings of echinaeas, salvias, perovskia, philadelphus, dianthus, phlomis, verbascums and stipa grasses. Different roses ('Kew Gardens', 'Malvern Hills', 'Ghislaine de Féligonde') grow on the wall against the moat and against the wall of the chapel (here *Rosa banksiae* var. *normalis*, *R.* x *odorata* 'Mutabilis', *R.* 'Souvenir du Docteur Jamain').

Despite its 'open' position at the corner of the house, by the moat, the garden as a whole feels enclosed, akin to being inside a richly decorated Arts and Crafts drawing room with polychrome tilework and wood carvings. But it does not prove to be indigestible or fatiguing, because Tom has employed the principle of rhythmic repetition of species across the planting beds.

'That's something I learned very early on,' Tom reflects. 'The first job I ever did was at Plumpton Place – a Lutyens house within a bit of a Jekyll garden. I worked there in the mid-1980s, a job that really came via Penny [Penelope Hobhouse]. When I had sent her the planting plans, she said to me: "You must repeat more. Simplify and repeat," she said. I remember that very well.'

On a practical note, the making of the garden presented particular challenges because of its position on an island surrounded by a moat. With no way in to the garden other than through the narrow doors of the house, a temporary bridge had to be constructed to bring machines, plants and building materials across the moat.

YOTES COURT

Previous pages
The view from the new pool building across the parterre to the house, a Jacobean building remodelled in the mid-17th century.

Above
The relationship between the new contemporary parterre and the modernist pool building is delineated on this eye-level sketch plan.

Opposite
The woodland garden, with cow parsley-like *Cenolophium denudatum* in the foreground and the purple spires of *Veronicastrum virginicum* 'Lavendelturm' beyond.

The historical documents may not be crystal clear, but there is evidence that a late 17th-century formal garden of avenues and parterres once complemented the red-brick, Grade I-listed mansion of 1656 at Yotes Court, in Kent. Tom used this as the basis for his notion of a garden of confident formality and simplicity that nevertheless contains within its compartments moments of intimacy and horticultural intensity. 'I wanted to make a contemporary garden that had echoes of the 17th century about it,' Tom explains. 'I felt there was a semi-Bridgemannick garden in there, trying to get out.' Charles Bridgeman was the leading landscape designer of the early 18th century, specializing in terraces and land form.

The garden is essentially a series of shallow platforms that descend towards the house, with a pronounced east–west lateral gradient too. The upper (north) end of the garden space was made into a walled garden in the late 18th century, and Tom has retained some sense of enclosure there, while removing a 4.5-metre (15-ft) tall holly hedge which bisected the garden.

'You could see the bones of an older garden beneath what was there,' Tom recalls. 'I thought it was important to try to connect the idea of the 17th-century garden to the contemporary – to make an asymmetrical formality.' This plan was made more urgent by the addition of a monumental modernist pool building by Sergison Bates Architects, just west of the house. 'I used to call it the Schinkel orangery,' Tom says, referring to the German neoclassical architect. 'It's not a subsidiary element,' he continues. 'So that now there were these two impossibly different buildings juxtaposed you needed a strong presence to provide both a

Previous pages
The parterre planting – persicaria, *Euphorbia cornigera*, *Salvia nemorosa* 'Amethyst', *Helenium* 'Moerheim Beauty' – with the pool building by Sergison Bates beyond.

Left
The fluffy plumes of perovskia add a textural note.

Opposite
The view back from the upper level of the walled garden, with box balls and alliums set amid hakonechloa grass.

link and a division between them, and in the process actually creating a greater sense of space.'

Tom's 'strong presence' takes the form of a series of tightly clipped box hedges that define narrow rectangular beds planted with a limited range of strong-coloured plants deployed in blocks, including *Salvia nemorosa* 'Amethyst', *Dianthus carthusianorum*, *Baptisia australis* and *Astrantia major* 'Claret', with masses of alliums in spring. The beds are geometrically arranged so that they form a powerful formal link between the house and the pool building. The result is quite cool, emotionally – more in the tradition of late 20th-century modernism (Geoffrey Jellicoe, Sylvia Crowe) than the contemporary style of naturalistic planting which Tom has used elsewhere. As he points out: 'The flower garden responds in a classical, parterre-like manner to the 17th-century building, and at the same time in quite a modernist way to the new building.' The modernist tone is continued just to the south, in the topiary garden of clipped yew forms which stand sentinel like cosmic chess-pieces.

North of the pool building lies one of the most successful parts of the new garden, a former shrubbery that is now an atmospheric wild garden of winding paths among maples, yews, pin and holm oaks, a tulip tree and a tall eucalyptus. Notable plants here include amsonias (*A. tabernaemontana* var. *salicifolia* and *A. hubrichtii*), *Euphorbia* 'Whistleberry Garnet', *Veronicastrum virginicum* 'Apollo', *Lunaria rediviva* and *Gillenia trifoliata*, with some judicious sprinklings of the grasses *Molinia caerulea* subsp. *arundinacea* 'Transparent' and *Miscanthus sinensis* 'Ferner Osten'.

Adjacent and to the east is a simple panel of lawn shaded by a large old oak, before the garden shifts up a level to the site of the walled garden. The western perimeter wall is heavily planted with a more woodland palette including hydrangeas (*H. paniculata* 'Tardiva', *H. serratifolia*, *H. heteromalla*), *Clerodendrum bungei*,

Campanula lactiflora 'Prichard's Variety', peonies, philadelphus, molinia grasses and several different varieties of *Clematis viticella*. Phloxes also do well here – 'Franz Schubert', 'Eventide' and 'Blue Paradise'.

The walled garden is divided into compartments with differing characters, including a nuttery of Kentish cobnuts, a vegetable garden, a cutting garden and a 'play lawn'. In addition there are formal elements such as a large panel of the grass *Calamagrostis brachytricha*, which creates a curiously agricultural moment. The grass is complemented by plantings of *Veronicastrum virginicum* 'Lavendelturm', *Helenium* 'Moerheim Beauty' and echinaceas, providing a strong sense of dynamic movement within the formal constraints.

Over the wall on the western side is a large orchard of mature trees, beneath which a wildflower meadow is allowed to grow long. A vibrant shrub border of lilacs, viburnums and many other species has been planted against the west-facing outer wall, and over on the eastern side is a spring border with irises, cranesbill geraniums, pulmonarias, epimediums, *Viburnum opulus* and roses.

The environs of the house have been treated relatively simply. The house had previously been a hotel possessed of what Tom describes as 'a rather depressing institutional feel', adding that much of the design work has been an attempt to recover from that. On the north side, giving on to the main garden, clipped box balls help define a garden terrace where *Phillyrea latifolia* grows in Versailles tubs, while the beds against the house contain *Hydrangea arborescens* 'Annabelle', *Penstemon* 'Raven' and *Euphorbia mellifera*. The north, entrance front faces the open park and its three huge old plane trees, with the front door flanked by roses and a pair of *Magnolia grandiflora*, with suitably scaled brackets of pleached lime to bookend the scene.

Previous pages
A grassy walk, dominated by *Miscanthus sinensis* 'Malepartus', with the original Jacobean gables of the house visible over the beech hedge.

Opposite
The upper part of the woodland garden, with *Cenolophium denudatum* and trees including *Acer palmatum*.

Right
The parterre seen from the lower exit of the woodland garden.

FORT BELVEDERE

Previous pages
This architectural confection, built as a mock fortification in Windsor Great Park, was erected in 1755 and further embellished in 1827–29.

Above
The setting of the building within the forested Windsor Great Park is clearly shown here, with vistas towards Virginia Water at top and left, and the main lake centre right. The area of woodland recently replanted with flowering trees and shrubs is at top left, against the curving bastion wall of the fort.

Opposite
A new oak gate to the Bombardier's Courtyard, festooned with wisteria.

This extraordinary Regency Gothic building, first constructed as a 'folly' in 1755 and then extended in 1827–29, was built to resemble a military installation. The tower surveys a landscape of more than 80 hectares (200 acres), most of which is woodland. In the early 1930s the house was famous (or perhaps notorious) as the home of the Duke of Windsor; he renovated both house and garden, employing the society planting designer Norah Lindsay to work on the borders. Ultimately, in 1936, the Duke had to relinquish 'the fort' after signing his abdication letter there, as Edward VIII. After several decades of neglect, the Crown leased out the property, and it remains in private hands today.

As with Oakhill, this is a site which Tom first worked at (for the same clients) while employed at Elizabeth Banks Associates, though his recent work on the estate has been far more extensive. Tom saw his essential task as lightening the overall feel, bringing something of the delicacy – even frothiness, in places – of Regency Gothic to the landscape, at a property which always has the capacity to appear slightly bleak, not least because of its quasi-militaristic bearing. To this end, Tom has added large flower borders around the front door, with white agapanthus in pots, roses (a Banksian and 'Cornelia') and a climbing hydrangea. The pots are terracotta, but were whitewashed to match the window frames, now a soft ochre as opposed to the previous cream.

The dense woodland was opened up through the removal of some 1,200 trees (mainly plantation pine, as well as an understorey of alder and laurel), while the environs of the lake to the north of the house were planted up with ferns, gunnera and darmera at the margins. This, together with a new shrub walk along its western

edge, means that the lake does not appear to sit as starkly in the scene as before. Tom's masterplan also links this northern, 'front' part of the estate with the other garden areas, which formerly felt somewhat detached.

'The big thing we have done is to make the landscape function radially,' Tom explains, 'linking the rhododendron woodland [to the east] with the lake and the valley garden [to the south]. It has now become a landscape which functions as a walking circuit.'

The lake itself sits in a mini-park, with blue cedars, metasequoia, liquidambars and tulip trees, while the eastern woodland has been augmented with numerous *Cornus kousa*, several varieties of prunus, rhododendrons, amelanchiers and a grove of katsura (*Cercidiphyllum*). In spring the area is lit up by narcissus and cowslips, and six weeks of continuous cherry blossom, since varieties have been chosen which flower in succession. It's all very much in the 'dell' style of the royal gardens of Windsor Great Park. 'I was hugely influenced by the Savill Garden,' Tom says. 'When I first went there I met John Bond, who had worked for [Eric] Savill and the Duke of Windsor. One does need to think of this as a component of the royal landscape. It's unfortunate that there is a busy road between it and Virginia Water now, but it is part of a continuum.'

Tom has emphasized this link by creating the Leg O'Mutton Pond in the dip directly south of the house, with a line of poplars beyond, which traces the (lost) historic vista towards Virginia Water. 'We put water down there almost to make it look as if it was part of the whole Virginia Water landscape,' he says. 'You get an intimation of what lies beyond.'

On the way down to the lake a vibrant cascade garden, with clear water splashing over rocks, is made out of an old alpine garden that was created by the Duke in the 1930s (reputedly bought 'off the shelf' at a garden show at Crystal Palace). 'We partially dismantled the rock garden to make it work as a cascade down the

Previous pages
Lemon trees and box topiaries in the swimming pool garden.

Left
The intimate Bombardier's Courtyard, with the flowers of *Libertia formosa*.

Opposite
The Fountain Garden, a new addition that includes an oak Gothic bench of Tom's design set amid white narcissus in long grass.

valley,' Tom says. 'It really does work and it was a fun thing to do.' There are tree ferns, yews, epimediums and some original azaleas higher up the slope, before it opens out to the lake, where candelabra primulas add some zing.

Tom has dignified the Duke's swimming pool with attractively over-sized clipped-box balls and citrus trees in tubs. Over to the east is the Belvedere Woodland, where some 500 trees have been removed and new pathways and tree plantings made. 'This is the bit which will be the best of the lot,' Tom says. 'In fifteen years' time it will really be something – we planted about 1,200 rhododendrons of all kinds and more than 300 trees [cornus, amelanchiers, beeches, pines, turkey oaks]. We are trying to initiate a more curatorial approach.'

The whole eastern and southern side of the building is 'defended' by decorative battlements which create the setting for a pair of 200-metre (650-ft) long parallel borders on two levels which were replanted by Rosemary Verey in the 1980s. Tom has retained the traditional feel, with roses, peonies, hydrangeas, erigeron, hypericums and other cottagey plants. 'I've never planted a mophead hydrangea in my life,' he says, 'but I felt it was important to retain these things as part of the story of the garden. You don't want to come in and erase everything.'

He has pursued a similarly respectful approach to the enclosed gardens lying west of and below the house, which were worked on by Arabella Lennox-Boyd in the 1990s: a potager and a rose garden, which Tom has remade into a wildflower meadow adorned with olive trees in terracotta pots. In addition, an empty enclosure was made into the Fountain Garden, where Tom designed the furniture, fountain and planting. Meanwhile, up on the lawn above the battlements is a reminder of the military conceit that underpins the place: a line of 31 brass cannon. These were formerly in the care of a bombardier in the Royal Artillery who had his own quarters adjacent to the main building.

Previous pages
Iris sibirica 'Papillon' and (darker) 'Shirley Pope' with camassias and *Euphorbia palustris*, by the Leg O'Mutton Pond.

Left
A glade in the extensive woodland which encircles the fort.

DESIGN PHILOSOPHY

Tim Richardson

Planting is only the final element – the 'icing on the cake' – of any landscape scheme. As Tom puts it: 'One of my objectives is for the overall experience to be one where the planting is reinforcing a character that is primarily made by the place and the space – the walls, the trees, the scale. I don't want the content of the planting to be so varied as to be too distracting or intimidating in its variety. The experience of the garden is the sum of the emotions you feel while going round the place, not an individual view.'

Tom is keenly aware of the abiding value of spontaneity and intuition in the creative process, and the danger of losing the initial, spontaneous design concept as a result of practical considerations over time, or simply over-thinking the matter. As he explains:

> I recall seeing a film about the Polish pianist Piotr Anderszewski in which he says that his best performances are when he is not aware of trying to play at all. The music flows. In music this is clearly something that is only possible after years of study – the technique and understanding of the music is to a great extent internalized. Perhaps the same is true in gardens. It is difficult to make a significant garden without an understanding of the cultural foundation on which a garden is made. But then it's often best to absorb and even forget that mass of information and attempt a more immediate and intuitive response to a place; not overly studied. Too often cleverness gets in the way of being able to show the story and the nature of a place clearly.

For this designer, then, the 'big picture' is always the most important facet of any design, as evinced by the fact that he literally creates a big picture at the beginning of each project: a large-scale pencil drawing of the entire scheme as envisaged, which is depicted in a wider landscape setting wherever appropriate. These meticulously prepared drawings preface the case-studies in this book. It is important to realize that in almost every instance they are completed before any work is begun, because the designer has worked out every detail of the scheme before any ground is disturbed.

Always there is a sense that Tom is attempting to identify and then enrich the natural character of a space. As he explains, what he wants to achieve is a 'cumulative impact of moving through a sequence of spaces, or giving a sense of how a garden connects a place to the complexities of its context, and for me these are often the most important aspects of my work in place making. With a number of gardens I feel that my greatest contribution has been to emphasize the sense of focus in a place and to find a language of design that gives meaning and a feeling of a garden being rooted in its physical and historical context.'

With private domestic commissions, this is usually informed as much by the personality of the owners as anything else. It's something of a cliché to suggest that designers 'psychoanalyse' their clients, but there is no doubt that the designer–client relationship can be emotionally and intellectually intense. As Tom states, however: 'I am not drawing a portrait of people. What you are trying to do is seize on some empathetic strand that connects you, so that your ideas might resonate with them.'

At Madresfield Court in Worcestershire, the clients wanted a small garden next to the house to become the main garden space for everyday use, with a mixture of terrace, lawn and abundant flowers. But this is no ordinary house. It has been in the same family since the 12th century, was significantly reconstructed in the late 19th century and contains a range of richly decorated rooms and structures, including a chapel that is one of the most complete painted Arts and Crafts interiors in Britain. The area Tom was to design is bordered on two sides by the moat and on the others by the house. The result is a secluded and private space which also looks out on to the wider garden and extensive parkland.

Tom is at pains to point out that the input of his clients into his garden designs is often of paramount importance; he is not a designer who pays lip service to this notion, but someone who is genuinely interested in other people – how they think, how they live their lives and how a garden might improve their day-to-day existence. It may sound slightly ridiculous or even over-privileged, but in many cases, when a client has reached a moment in their lives where they have the

Detail of the aerial drawing proposal for the moat garden at Madresfield Court.

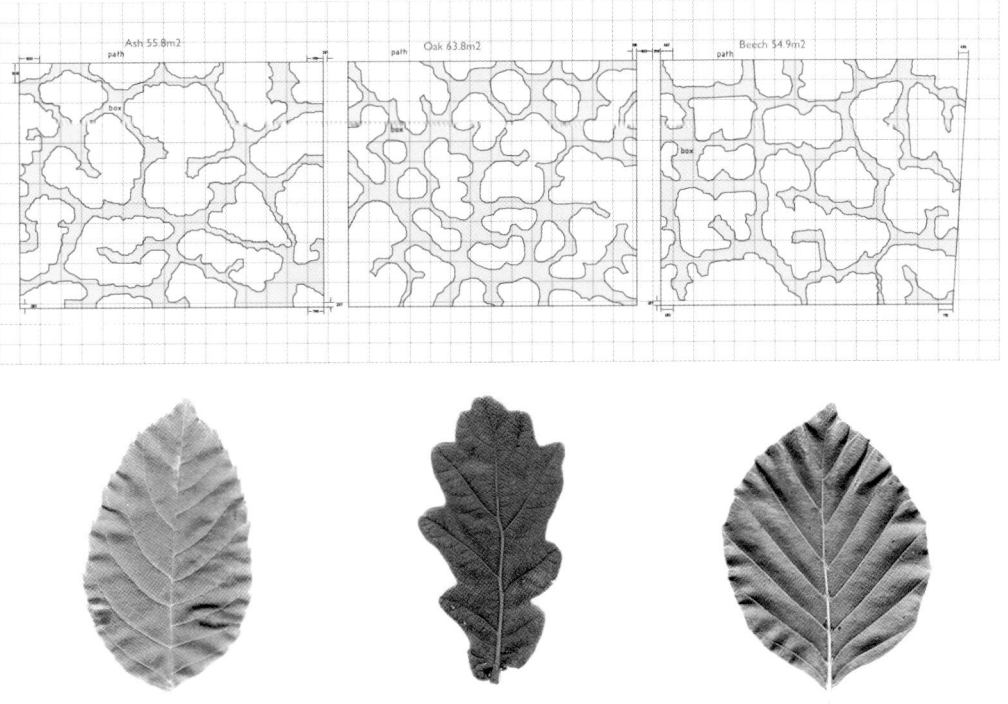

Leaves of ash, oak and beech from trees around the proposed site of the garden at Broughton Grange. Above is the pattern formed by their cells revealed under a microscope. This then became the hedge layout in the parterre.

time and resources to commission someone like Tom, they are at a turning point, having made their money or achieved much of what they wanted. A garden can then become emblematic of this next phase of life.

On a more down-to-earth level, Tom thinks deeply about the materials to be used in addition to the planting – elements such as walls, hedges and topiary used for structure. As well as following his intuition as a designer, gleaned from on-site visits and conversations with clients, Tom pursues rigorous historical research where appropriate, and also commissions scientific studies into the endemic flora of the region and how it might be complemented. Whether the site is a small private garden on the north Norfolk coast in the UK, or an extensive, multi-use compound in Kerala, India, this agenda is pursued with exactly the same level of rigour and application. In Tom's methodology history, science, psychology, ecology and creative design are all given equal weight.

Often he finds some detail of ancient land use or natural features as the springing off point for a design, sometimes from unexpected sources. The large parterre on the lower terrace at Broughton Grange is a case in point, as Tom describes: 'It is the most abstract part of the whole composition and, on the face of it, quite disengaged from the surrounding landscape. It is planted with box and appears like a carpet of vacuoles, suggesting something cellular and organic, and is in fact a magnification of the cell pattern in the leaves of the trees in the surrounding hedgerows: beech, oak and ash. So while in one respect the design is remote from the landscape, there is a connection at a microscopic level. The parterre is like an offering up of nature to nature.'

At Mount St John, Tom first viewed the project he was to embark on from the roof of the house, surveying the landscape of fields and hedgerows stretched out like a patchwork quilt. In his research, as he says, he

took a closer look at the historic maps and realized that although the landscape from a distance looks unchanged, it was actually thinning out rapidly. In the view from the house, over half of the hedges and hedgerow trees have disappeared since the first edition of the Ordnance Survey in 1870, at which time the Vale of York would have appeared

DESIGN PHILOSOPHY

Plan for the Italianate garden at Trentham. This drawing also shows an early plan by Piet Oudolf to the east (right) of it.

from our vantage point like a forest wilderness rather than an agricultural landscape. In a move to remember that apparent wilderness I took the pattern of hedges from the section of the 1870 plan that we see in the view today and imposed them as a print over the ground at the point where the garden meets the landscape, using tall grasses to form the lines bisecting other types of plants. So what you see is an abstraction of the landscape as it was, laid out in front of the landscape as it now is.

Part of the restoration programme of Sir Charles Barry's monumental Italianate garden at Trentham was bringing the vast 4-hectare (10-acre) parterre originally designed by the mid-19th-century garden designer William Andrews Nesfield back to life. A map also provided a source here, but in a more subversive way:

> The replanting style was consciously opposed to anything that Barry and Nesfield would have approved of. But I did feel a strong desire to fix the planting in this place. Thinking back to the origins of the estate on the river and its importance in the fortunes of Trentham I turned to thinking about the place of water and streams in the 19th-century imagination and how for the Romantics the stream was often used as a symbol for various aspects of the inner life, for lost love, the free spirit, the passing of time and endless desire. It was a wonderfully flexible symbol that could be used for just about anything in the world of the imagination – a different universe to the authoritarian fixity of Barry's great scheme.

So over the whole extent of the parterre I planted a web of tall grasses that are an accurate plan of the River Trent and its tributaries at a scale of 1:800, stretched over the garden like a net. In the winter, when some of the other planting dies back, this pattern is clearly visible – if you know what you are looking for. I like to think of it as a quiet subversion of the imperialist, autocratic world view that created this astonishing garden in the first place, ideas which are now so out of tune with the way most of us see the world.

The project for a house at Kottayam, in Kerala, southern India, presented a different sort of challenge. As Tom explains of the work of his studio there: 'In many respects what we have done is not make a garden. Instead we have used traditional techniques of husbandry and water management to organize the place and a garden-like quality has followed.'

He continues:

Almost all the work is done by hand. The paving is made from polygonal granite blocks cut by hand by masons who come from a dynasty of masons going back beyond memory. The water channels are dug by men stripped down to a *lungi* who seem impervious to what might be slithering around in the bottom of the ditch.

It is possible to enumerate certain 'trademarks' of the Tom Stuart-Smith approach. These include the use of grids of rectangular beds which in practice, in season, merge to create the impression of one large area of planting. Clipped evergreen shapes, topiaries and groups of small trees (notably cornus, malus, hornbeam and rhus) are also used to create a subtle sense of structure, either close to the house, as an independent element within a larger geometric design, or to help anchor a view a little further out. Topiary has more of a presence in some of Tom's earlier schemes (notably at Broughton), lending the work something of the appeal of the style of Arts and Crafts planting designer Norah Lindsay, though now Tom says he has the confidence to use less rather than more evergreen material.

In terms of 'hard' materials, Tom likes to create simple, powerful effects by using materials such as diamond-sawn stone or metal panels, to emphasize what he calls 'the static, geometric quality of the constructed part of the garden'. This will often be contrasted with something much more textural, such as cobblestones or river pebbles.

He almost always uses British stone – preferably local – with York stone the default material of choice. 'There is no use of ornament – unless there is an established precedent – and very little use of sculpture to highlight axes or "direct" the view,' Tom explains. 'In the earlier work, particularly – for example at Broughton Grange and Mount St John – I saw the built structure of the garden as an unchanging,

Aerial view of Culham Court, showing the terraces which descend to the River Thames (at lower right) and the swimming pool garden (left).

crystalline imposition or constraint on the land, and the planting as the disruptive antithesis to this. I now see the whole less as a dialectic and more of a synthetic composition.'

Corten steel has also been favoured (though again, less so now), used to create an agricultural, textural feel and to play off certain plants, notably grasses; it is primarily used for structural devices such as panel walls to portion up space, or as narrow water tanks.

Water is indeed a constant presence in Tom's designs, generally used as a still centre or 'void' at the heart of a geometric scheme or terraced garden. 'It is the ultimate texture,' Tom remarks. 'Water has this uncanny quality of being both an absence and a presence. I am much more interested in still water than I am in moving water, though lots of people pine for it in their gardens. In the end, I really just want a still reflecting pool. It often constitutes a kind of resolution in the composition.'

A still pool or canal-like rectangle of water will often be an element in one of Tom's tripartite walled gardens (as at Culham Court, Cogshall Grange and Middleton Lodge). He describes these – instinctively using a musical analogy – as constituted of 'two contrasting outer parts with a resolving middle section'. Tom has made quadripartite schemes, but says these can tend towards fragmentation unless they are realized on a very large scale, as at Encombe's walled garden. Such structural and spatial elements, often played off against naturalistic planting, are key to creating the sense of dynamic contrast which Tom is always seeking to engender in his designs.

Encombe lies in a deep, sheltered and enclosed valley, and the 1.2-hectare (3-acre) walled garden is itself like another world within. Tom explains his ideas behind this garden within a garden:

In thinking about the potential for making a garden here I was reminded of the Greek myth in which Zeus unleashes two eagles at opposite ends of the earth. The two birds meet at Delphi, where he places a stone called the Omphalos to mark the centre, or navel, of the world. It seemed that the centre of the walled garden could be such a place, if only in the smaller world of Encombe. So we decided to mark the centre of the garden by a

Initial design drawing for the walled garden at Encombe. It shows the concept of the 'garden within a garden'.

Design proposal drawing for the Islamic Garden at Le Jardin Secret, Marrakech.

rough stone fountain. A link to the deep spirit of the place. This sits at the centre of a small formal quartered garden surrounded by a low yew hedge and this is surrounded by a meadow planted with fruit trees which itself is enclosed by the high wall of the garden. So there is a sense of ever increasing detail and focus as we approach the centre of this landscape. With layer after layer of enclosure, the garden has an extraordinary sense of emplacement; of being deeply rooted and enfolded in that golden bowl of hills and woods. The garden layout itself is a simple, timeless, quadripartite plan that directly recalls the enclosed Islamic garden at Le Jardin Secret in Marrakech and countless other gardens that have gone before and since.

At Le Jardin Secret in Marrakech both the presence of water and a quadripartite layout were integral to the project. Here two riads, traditional Moroccan houses with blank walls facing the exterior and inner courtyard gardens, had been joined together in the late 19th century, and both had fallen into decay and been built over. The project was to restore and recast this historic garden in the heart of the Medina. Of this unusual scheme Tom comments that it was 'like all Islamic gardens, designed around water as the source and origin of life, and the central symbolic focus of the composition. Water is seen as the source of all organic growth and a symbol of God's mercy. We have tried to restore the water workings of the garden, or where this is not possible, at least to illustrate how the water mechanics of the garden worked and how the detailed design of the garden was entirely predicated on the gravitational movement of water.'

In the smaller of the two original properties it became apparent that the structure of the original garden had survived beneath the ground: 'One could see exactly where the former pavilion had stood and how a water channel ran from a basin in front of this building, down a central path to another basin within a building facing it at the other end of the garden. It was a layout not dissimilar to that of the Patio de la Acequia in the Generalife [Granada, Spain] but with a narrower and continuous central rill. So we redesigned the garden to work with the structures that had now been discovered.'

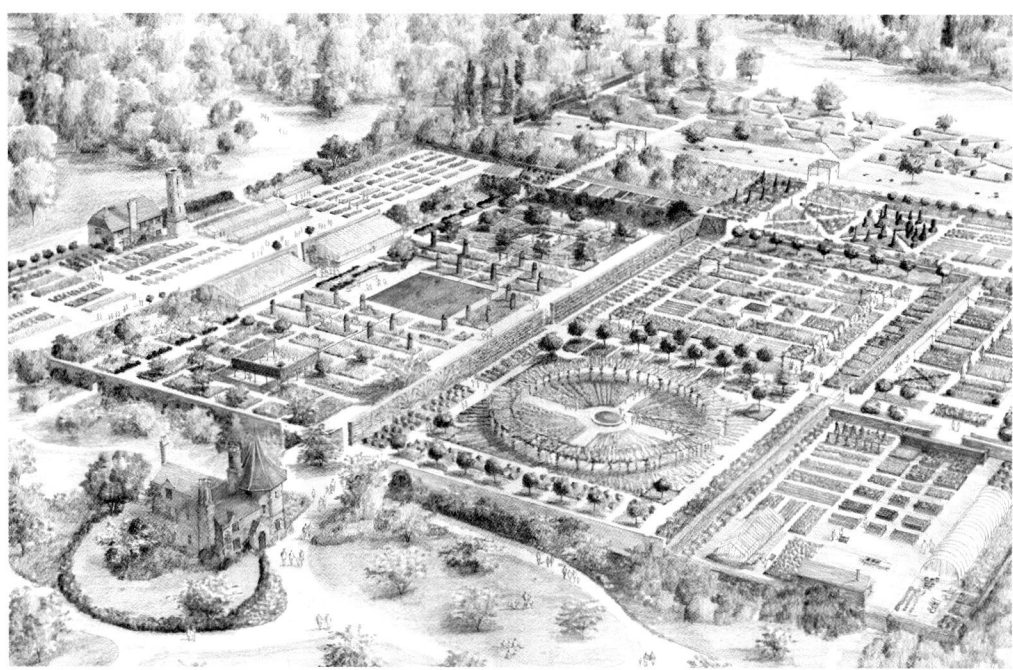

Preliminary design drawing for the left-hand enclosure of the paradise garden at RHS Bridgewater, with the central water basin.

The idea of the pool as the void at the heart of a garden emerges as an important touchstone, playing into Tom's continuing exploration of the nature of the designer–client relationship. Who can claim true ownership of the garden? How didactic should the designer be? Can the garden be permitted to retain some of its own secrets?

'I like the idea of the centre of the composition being something that you can look into, but you can't actually be in,' Tom says. 'I learnt this by doing the pool at Broughton – the very first one I made. The centre is something that cannot be occupied, so as a result there is a sense that you are always walking around the edges, looking in. The garden and the process of the garden, its momentum, you might say, then take precedence. The garden is not an anthropocentric composition, it is a thing in itself, that works to its own rules.' The concept of a central water basin has been reprised again recently in the design for the paradise garden at RHS Bridgewater.

For Tom, this sensation of looking over his own work dispassionately and objectively is reminiscent of his experiences as a zoologist studying animal behaviour, or even performing anatomical dissection. It allows him to step back from the work and in a sense relinquish control and ownership of what he has made. Because, ultimately, he has to walk away from any garden he has designed, which then takes on a life of its own. In common with most other designers, he will return on a consultancy basis wherever possible, but there will inevitably be changes to the planting as it matures and develops. The unoccupied space at the centre, on the other hand, remains a constant, unchanging presence – a zone of mediation between Tom and his client, and the garden, and perhaps even nature itself.

Scale

TRENTHAM

OAKHILL

RHS WISLEY

LE JARDIN SECRET

MOUNT ST JOHN

TRENTHAM

TRENTHAM

Previous pages
At this historic 19th-century garden, Tom rejuvenated a vast Italianate parterre with plantings of mainly perennials and grasses such as *Miscanthus sinensis* 'Gracillimus' (right).

Above
A low-perspective view of the Italian Garden or main parterre, with a long enclosing border designed by Piet Oudolf in the foreground.

Opposite
The structure of paths and fountain pools was left intact, while formal elements such as the columnar Irish yews were reprised.

A great Victorian Italianate garden spanning 4 hectares (10 acres) – the largest such parterre to be made anywhere in Britain – was by the late 1990s crying out for restoration. 'When I first saw the garden, it was sad,' Tom recalls. 'The Irish yews, intended by [the architect] Charles Barry to resemble Italian cypresses, looked more like Vietnamese pot-bellied pigs, while buddleias sprouted from the orangery and decaying garden temples.'

Despite its dilapidation, Trentham, in Staffordshire, still boasted perhaps the finest setting of any landscape garden in England: a mile-long lake modelled by 'Capability' Brown in the late 18th century, prefaced by the huge parterre and surrounded by the low, wooded hills of an estate of 305 hectares (750 acres).

In the late 19th century Trentham had been one of England's great houses, the seat of the Leveson-Gower family, dukes of Sutherland. The second duke oversaw the rebuilding of the house, between 1834 and 1847, to elegant Italianate designs by Barry (who later collaborated with Augustus Pugin on the Houses of Parliament). But the house was dynamited in 1912 after the family had abandoned the estate because of pollution in the River Trent, which fed the water for the fountains in the parterre. All that survived were some dislocated remnants such as loggias, the forlorn remains of the house and the structure of the parterre itself. For a while it was a popular public amenity and venue (the Beatles even played there), but by 1996, when it was bought by property development company St Modwen, it had sunk into dilapidation, with not a single gardener employed.

By that time the shine was also just beginning to wear off the 'restoration mania' which had been sweeping the British heritage garden scene during the preceding

Left
In autumn and winter the colour tones from the grasses and perennial plants such as sedums are just as vibrant as the late summer scene.

Opposite
Mist rises from the lake in the distance, with clipped Portuguese laurels in Versailles tubs flanking the central path.

decade and had resulted in scores of historic gardens and parks being studiously brought back to something like their original form. So instead of doing the obvious thing, which would have been to restore the parterres to their formal glory using thousands, even millions, of bedding plants and annual flowers, St Modwen decided to pursue a more contemporary treatment. The idea was to resurrect Trentham as a 'country park' open to the public, but also to make it into a new garden of national if not international significance. It took them seven years of planning and other battles to get the project off the ground, but when it was completed it was almost universally adjudged a success.

That it has succeeded is largely due to the key personnel engaged on the project: Tom, who was asked to redesign the parterres, and leading historic landscape consultant Dominic Cole, who took on aspects of the wider landscape. Tom, in turn, asked planting designer Piet Oudolf to contribute planting designs for certain discrete areas (there was no material overlap in their creative input – which suited them both). The management of the entire estate was then undertaken by head gardener Michael Walker, who was recruited from Waddesdon Manor.

The smaller, upper parterre – square in form – was in fact restored in conventional manner so that it appears like a Victorian parterre design of the 1850s, with colourful and seasonally changing displays of bulbs, annuals, biennials and exotics. It forms a suitable complement to the orangery, the most intact surviving element of Barry's architecture.

The much larger lower parterre was entirely Tom's domain, where his aim was to re-present the gardens in a contemporary manner while staying true to the theatrical grandiloquence that was part of the historic appeal. This was always a festive, social space, designed to delight and amuse visitors as well as the family who lived there (for a small part of the year). It seems fitting that it is open to the public daily.

Tom's response was to enlarge the beds and to replant them in his own style. 'On the upper levels, where the drainage is good, it is more German steppe or dry meadow planting, with an intermingled tapestry of plants,' he explains. 'We kept the soil fairly lean and mean here.' Accordingly, Tom utilized a more 'Mediterranean' palette – salvias, euphorbias, phlomis, rudbeckia, as well as more than fifty varieties of bearded iris – making for a lighter-coloured scheme and a more open feel.

This is big-sweep gardening, in accordance with the setting, but there is also plenty of detail, with verbascums, echinaceas, cirsiums, dahlias, eremurus and alliums mingling with bronze fennel. Certain plants create tonal and textural counterpoints at different moments in the season: the dark umbels of sedums offsetting the yellows and oranges, lime-green euphorbias adding a little zing to moodier moments, and the bearded irises making a show in springtime. Plants are generally deployed in groups to create drifts, or else repeated within individual beds, so that the visitor does not feel too absorbed by any single area of planting in this vast space.

Then there are the grasses, which emphasize rhythm and unity in so many of Tom's projects. 'Over the whole extent of the parterre I planted a web of tall grasses that read like a network of tenacious roots,' he explains. 'In fact they are a representation of the River Trent and all its tributaries, stretched over the garden like a net.' Tom went as far as to overlay a scale map of these tributaries across a plan of the parterre, tracing the course of the rivers with his plantings of miscanthus and pennisetum.

The lower parterre slopes down towards the lake at its south end. A range of larger, more moisture-tolerant plants were used in the richer soil here, including *Eupatorium purpureum*, *Veronicastrum virginicum* 'Lavendelturm' and *Thalictrum rochebruneanum*. The healthiness of the plants is testament to the preparation of the soil in the parterre, which was entirely replaced. All of this is framed within the vocabulary of formal Victorian gardening: seven large fountain pools, spires of Irish yew, clipped Portuguese laurels in Versailles tubs, balustrading and numerous restored or replaced urns.

At the foot of the lower parterre, by the lake, is a bronze copy of Benvenuto Cellini's *Perseus and Medusa* (around 1550), from the Loggia dei Lanzi in Florence – a perfect endnote, with the muscled hero holding aloft the head of the gorgon, his sword gripped in his other hand. Across the lake at its far, southern end, a statue of the 1st Duke still stands on Monument Hill, surveying a garden which has been given a contemporary function and meaning.

Previous pages
Winter in the parterre, with the elegant stems of *Stipa gigantea* and the vermilion caps of *Hylotelephium* 'Munstead Dark Red'.

Opposite
Two statues overlook the lake: a fine copy of Benvenuto Cellini's *Perseus and Medusa* and in the distance, more than a mile away, atop a column, a statue of the 1st Duke of Sutherland.

OAKHILL

Previous pages
Dawn over the American meadows, with species including *Echinacea pallida* and *E. paradoxa*, and *Silphium laciniatum* and *S. terebinthinaceum*.

Above
The relationship between newly planted areas, ponds and the contemporary office buildings is delineated in this drawing. The original Oak Hill House is at centre right. The prairies stretch away beyond the offices, at the top of the drawing

Opposite
The garden is surprisingly 'wild' for a corporate setting – here, tall *Eupatorium purpureum* backs *Sanguisorba officinalis* 'Red Thunder' and Japanese anemones to create an informal woodland feel.

A large corporate headquarters was an unusual commission for Tom Stuart-Smith's office to undertake, but in this case there was a compelling reason. The then chairman of the financial services corporation, was, in Tom's words, 'nuts about gardens'. He envisaged a strong horticultural and design component to the office complex, though this being a business environment, there were of course a few strings attached. There was to be no formality whatsoever, and an underlying oriental theme expressed by means of Chinese urns, statuary and specimen tree and shrub plantings – mainly acers, cornus, zelkova and nandina.

The estate at Oakhill is chiefly agricultural land, but at its heart lies some 8 hectares (20 acres) of garden around Oak Hill House, an early 19th-century, Grade II-listed neoclassical villa, with an associated dower house. The setting had been compromised over the years by the addition of a variety of large office buildings of varying architectural quality, as well as car parks and other facilities.

This is something of a recurring project for Tom, who first worked on this site in the late 1980s while employed at Elizabeth Banks Associates, only to return later to refresh the design in his own right. The basis for this second phase of work was the idea of episodic complexity around the buildings, giving way to expansive meadow and prairie plantings. 'It's an old Victorian pleasure ground, and that really comes through,' Tom begins. Indeed, his fairly intense plantings of shrubs, small trees and drifting perennials might be said to constitute a modernist shrubbery aesthetic. 'Virtually everything that didn't need to be open space ended up being planted,' he explains. 'The buildings are so lacking in unity that they needed a lot of context, in terms of the planting, to make them hang together at all.' Key plants in the areas around the buildings include *Hydrangea quercifolia*, epimediums, phlomis, the grasses *Molinia caerulea* subsp. *caerulea* 'Poul Petersen' and hakonechloa, oriental hellebores and loosely clipped groups of box.

The old manor house, which has been used as accommodation for visiting staff and clients, sits to one side of the small modern reception building, which together with a curving link building forms a three-sided courtyard. 'The entrance court is based on the simple concept of maples with hakonechloa growing beneath,' Tom says. A specimen *Cornus controversa* by the entrance creates a calming horizontal mood by means of its branch structure, while a pair of Chinese lion guardian statues contributes to the oriental theme. The branches of the acers and other trees here have been lifted to allow for views and dappling shade.

On the north and south sides of the office complex the shrubbery character of the garden is especially apparent. To the south is an area known as Reception Lawn, where a grove of gleditsia is focused on *Warp and Weft* (2003), a sculpture by Peter Randall-Page. This is a tightly composed, self-contained garden episode, with snowdrops, scillas and crocuses appearing in spring. Adjacent is a small pond surrounded by existing laurels, philadelphus, prunus and other older shrubs which have been reduced and brightened by plantings of *Euphorbia characias* subsp. *wulfenii*, groups of small-leaved box 'Faulkner', *Skimmia* x *confusa* 'Kew Green' and, against the buildings, vivid pink-flowered *Camellia sasanqua*, the evergreen *Clematis armandii* 'Apple Blossom', *Ligustrum lucidum*, wisteria and loquats.

Winding paths lead around the south of the building past more shrubbery plantings and specimen trees (magnolias, paulownias, *Cercis canadensis*, *Cornus alba* 'Sibirica') underplanted with geraniums, epimediums and molinia grass. The staff-restaurant terrace on the eastern side is dotted with bronze Chinese urns and maples (*Acer palmatum*), prunus and zelkova, with generous plantings of epimediums and hakonechloa below.

Left
The plumes of veronicastrum and one of the sculptures (this piece is by Jon Isherwood) which have been sited across the designed landscape.

Opposite
The vertical stems of *Verbena bonariensis* and veronicastrum beyond, with part of the original Oak Hill House visible.

Opposite
The walk from the car park to the main building is a landscape experience in its own right, with a variety of trees set amid swathes of hakonechloa.

Right
One of the paths that circles the main building, with *Phlomis russeliana* in the foreground and *Hemerocallis* 'Corky' opposite it.

The shrubbery walk on the north side of the building is one of the quietest but most effective aspects of the design, where a taller layer of *Hydrangea paniculata*, *Euphorbia* 'Whistleberry Garnet' and *Veronicastrum virginicum* 'Spring Dew' complements the subtle charms of astrantias, *Vinca minor* and *Epimedium rubrum*. Small groups of birches add to the elegant tone. This walk leads round to the west side of the building and the dower house (now self-contained flats) with adjacent pond, originally dug by the Romans as a marl pit. The pond has been extended to form a figure-of-eight shape, with marginal plantings of gunnera, *Darmera peltata*, *Miscanthus sinensis* 'Roland' and *Iris sibirica* 'Papillon'.

Tom worked with renowned horticultural ecologist James Hitchmough on the meadows and prairies at Oakhill. The main area of meadow planting is to the east of the office complex, where the garden meets the wider landscape. This part of the estate has the character of parkland, with clumps of horse chestnut and oak framing views over the fields. An 'American prairie' was created on a bed of clay and crushed concrete, itself thinly spread over the roof of a vast underground 'data centre'. The plant palette includes *Rudbeckia missouriensis*, *Dianthus carthusianorum*, *Echinacea* species, penstemons, oenothera and *Phlox pilosa*. In the early years *Silphium laciniatum* was found to be too dominant and had to be reduced.

'In some cases an exotic meadow will not sit happily with another type of planting which has a recognizable style,' Tom comments. 'A meadow looks best when it has something entirely neutral and unstylized next to it.' Another meadow planting is of the 'wetter' variety, with plants such as *Liatris ligulistylis*, *Geum triflorum*, *Gillenia trifoliata* and *Rudbeckia maxima*. Snakeshead fritillaries appear in spring.

As Tom concludes: 'The guiding principle is picturesque composition, and also an effort to keep the scale as human and domestic as possible ... At the time I was involved, there were more than 500 people working there and it did not feel like it. To me this project showed the value of designing in a cared-for place. I like the idea that perhaps if an institution cares for the place it inhabits, that philosophy extends to the way it looks after its employees, and vice versa.'

RHS WISLEY

RHS WISLEY

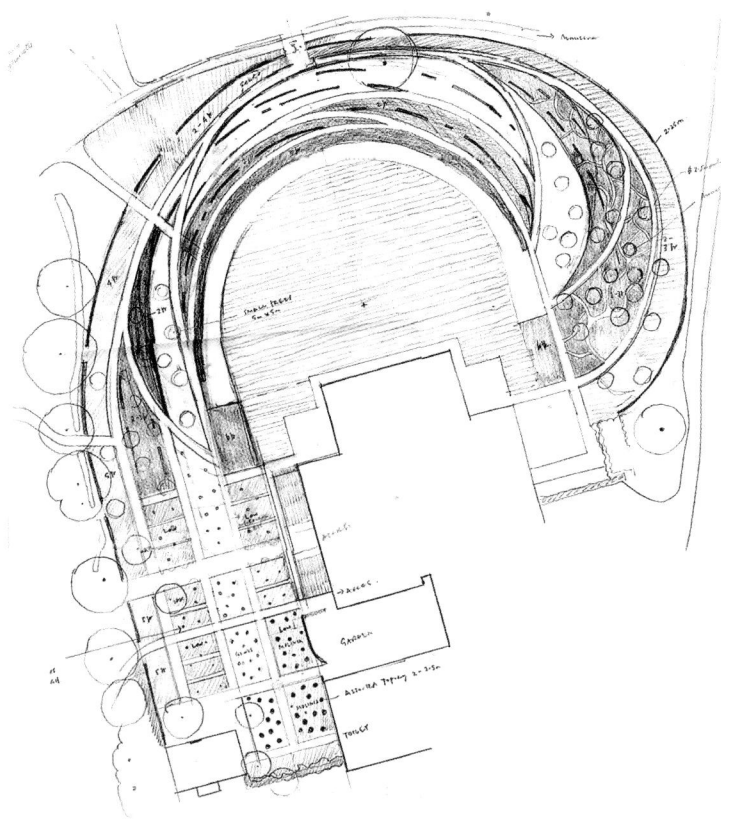

Previous pages
The main glasshouse at Wisley, where Tom's ground plan describes a huge semicircular arc, following the shape of the reservoir.

Above
The sheer scale of this project, which is some 160 metres (525 feet) across, can be appreciated in this sketch plan. The planting beds form an arc around the semicircular pond above the large glasshouse.

Opposite
The planting has a rhythmic pulse, with repeats of species such as *Stipa calamagrostis*, *Echinacea purpurea* 'Magnus' (both in the foreground) and *Eupatorium maculatum* 'Purple Bush'.

This project is remarkable not least for the speed with which it was undertaken – just seven months from inception until the moment the new glasshouse was opened by HM The Queen in June 2007. The haste has left the RHS with a few long-lasting issues around weed control, which are being addressed gradually and systematically by fallowing areas of planting in sequence in order to eradicate bindweed and horsetail. Another issue to contend with was that the site began as an open field – a very muddy open field, since the land here is wet to the point of waterlogging. The only 'givens' at the outset were the presence of the glasshouse –a perfectly serviceable 'off-the-shelf' product, despite its huge size – and the elongated semicircle of water in front of it, on its south side. This body of water doubles as the main reservoir for the garden and its plants.

A sense of place was created by means of long, ribbon-like beds and lines of hedges. The design follows the shape of the pool in a series of wide concentric arcs made up of richly planted beds of perennials, a central band of lawn dotted with trees (notably *Cornus kousa* and *Prunus yedoensis*) and pathways. The basic shape is further reinforced by broken lines of beech hedges, which also help to create a sense of enclosure. The scale of the ensemble demanded simple, muscular planting in the bed immediately adjacent to the water. This scheme was based on a palette of just five reliable species ('big chunks and endless repetition', as Tom puts it): *Veronicastrum virginicum* 'Fascination', *Eupatorium maculatum* 'Purple Bush', *Miscanthus sinensis* 'Ferner Osten', *Euphorbia cornigera* and *Helenium* 'Moerheim Beauty'.

Previous pages
The sun sets over the garden, with the cone flowers of echinaceas in the foreground.

Opposite
Sculptural beech topiaries lend a note of formality to the environs of the glasshouse entrance, with *Miscanthus sinensis* 'Starlight' in the foreground and prunus varieties behind offset by *Molinia caerulea* subsp. *arundinacea* 'Transparent'.

Right
The drier, western part of the garden, with *Panicum virgatum* 'Hänse Herms', echinaceas and *Hylotelephium* 'Matrona'.

On the east side of the glasshouse is the entrance, which visitors reach either via the copse known as Oakwood, or from the south, having walked down Dutch planting designer Piet Oudolf's long double borders (made in 2000). This eastern entrance side is the most formal part of the design, prefaced as it is with small 'fields' of miscanthus grass in combination with individual, scattered clipped beech cylinders, an arrangement constituting a fanfare of sorts for the glasshouse itself.

From here the line of the paths and planting beds leads the visitor south and then west around the pool, following a carefully organized 'narrative journey'. As with other projects, including Trentham and Mount St John, the planting components and the spatial design come together to create a strong sense of movement and progression. In this case, the trajectory is circular, as the visitor route follows an arc from the wetter, eastern side of the building to the drier western zone.

One early formulation of the plan was inspired by C-S-R triangle theory. The use of this evolutionary concept – associated with Universal Adaptive Strategy Theory – arose from Tom's scientific education and interests. The theory posits the survival of genes through competition (C), stress-tolerance (S) and rapid (or ruderal) gene propagation (R). 'I was thinking that one could start off with big groups of colonizing plants in fertile soils,' Tom explains, 'and then as you went around this great sweep you would end up with small groups of inter-meshed plants, with much more diversity and higher stress resulting from less fertile soil and drier conditions. It worked because around the wild garden [to the east] there is more shade and moisture, whereas the situation on the other [western] side is much drier.'

The perennial planting on the eastern side includes plants such as *Miscanthus sinensis* 'Kleine Silberspinne', *Salvia nemorosa* 'Amethyst', *Phlox paniculata* 'Franz Schubert', *Sanguisorba canadensis* and *Rodgersia pinnata* 'Superba', with an underpinning of hostas (*H. ventricosa* and *H. sieboldiana* var. *elegans*), epimediums and pulmonarias, masses of irises in spring and hellebores for winter. As the beds arc round to the southern side, this scheme gives way to more 'Mediterranean' plantings of euphorbias, sedums, thalictrums, digitalis, bearded irises, *Eremurus stenophyllus*, *Amsonia hubrichtii* and *Phlomis russeliana*. The grass mix also becomes more dramatic, with *Pennisetum alopecuroides* 'Moudry', *Carex testacea*, *Stipa calamagrostis* and *S. extremiorientalis*. The drier, more sunshine-oriented theme intensifies moving westwards around the pond, with drifts of cone-flowered echinaceas plus rudbeckias, teucriums, verbascums and panicum grasses. Finally, at the western (exit) side of the glasshouse, the visitor encounters a rectangular arid bed, with grevilleas, cistus, *Gomphostigma virgatum* and *Melianthus major* providing the structure for groups of kniphofias, crocosmias, salvias, agapanthus and *Alchemilla erythropoda*.

'Here at Wisley, where the audience is so knowledgeable, I was making a special effort not to make the plant groupings too big, and to emphasize the combinations,' Tom explains. 'The path pattern is on a spiral geometry and the hedges and the lake were on a radial geometry. I came up with this idea of two overlapping geometries as I was thinking about fugal structure.'

Musical analogies have long been a part of Tom's design process, and this train of thought proved particularly fruitful with this project. 'I designed this in one of my "Bach obsessive winters",' he reveals, 'when I was listening to nothing but Bach cantatas. I was thinking about fugues a lot. I am slightly obsessed by fugues ... Like *The Art of the Fugue* [by J.S. Bach], this design has this one beautiful strand starting, then another following, ending with a great semi-chaotic pile-up. That was the idea: to start very simple and orthogonal, then gradually build it up until the whole thing falls apart.'

Needless to say, most decorously.

Left
Achilleas and phlomis seedheads in the western part of the garden.

Opposite
Large clumps of miscanthus and other grasses have a bold structural presence all through the winter, until they are finally cut down in February.

LE JARDIN SECRET

It is something of a clichéd view in international landscape design that English landscape designers somehow remain stuck in the rut of Arts and Crafts and can only design traditional 'English' gardens. Le Jardin Secret in Marrakech, Morocco, shows that Tom Stuart-Smith has the ability to work in a variety of regional and historical idioms, while also maintaining his own distinctive identity as a designer.

'In this project, more than any other, I have been aware of the responsibility of working within another culture about which I am largely ignorant,' Tom reflects. 'Making a garden here has meant walking a narrow line between post-colonial pastiche on one side, and potentially dry historicism on the other.'

The first thing to understand about this garden is its extraordinary situation, right in the middle of the crowded lanes and bazaars of the Medina, or old walled city. This makes the oasis-like feel of these spaces, filled as they are with greenery and water, seem even more remarkable – indeed, almost miraculous, on a boiling hot day. As Tom comments, 'Much of the beauty and subtlety of Marrakech lies within the riads and palaces, unseen by most of us.'

Le Jardin Secret is the name given to a pair of courtyard gardens that originally belonged to separate properties. In the space of a year, Tom created two contrasting garden spaces: the Islamic Garden, a cruciform design on traditional Islamic lines, with plantings based on those mentioned in the Koran; and the Exotic Garden, a more intimate space, using plants sourced from all over the world.

When Tom arrived, the site was covered in rubble, rubbish and a variety of shacks and small dwellings, reflecting the fact the property was formerly in the ownership

Previous pages
One of the quarters of the larger, Islamic Garden, centred on a fountain pool, with olive trees and emerald-tiled pathways.

Above
A drawn visualization of the Exotic Garden. In this case all the plants and trees have been rendered with botanical accuracy.

Opposite
The Exotic Garden, with a central rill leading from the entrance hall.

Left
The cruciform layout of the Islamic Garden, as seen from the tower.

Opposite
Fluffy *Stipa tenuissima* grass, joined here by the native *Lavandula pinnata* and pink star-flowered *Tulbaghia violacea*.

of more than 130 people. The larger Islamic Garden had been the centrepiece of one of the most important houses in the city, thought to date back to the late 16th century, while the Exotic Garden belonged to a smaller adjacent property. Both were riads, an Arabic word which means 'house with garden'. They had been joined together in the late 19th century to form a single palace. The restoration process revealed that the original layout of paths and water-rills was still intact and clearly discernible. This layout was excavated and the rills put back into action.

Tom's original ideas for the smaller, Exotic Garden, which the visitor encounters first, were made before any archaeological evidence had come to light. 'Our initial design proposal was based on the idea of making an exotic and colourful garden, a post-colonial piece of exotically planted orientalism, designed for colour and sensual extravagance, in contrast to the more serene and spiritual character of the larger space,' he explains. But after it was discovered that the former layout of the garden had survived beneath the ground, Tom redesigned the garden to take this into account. The central rill was restored, as was a slightly raised perimeter walkway.

Intensively planted beds in irregular rectangles were recreated on either side of the rill, where Tom's planting features carefully engineered contrasts in form, colour and texture – for example between floppy kalanchoes ('elephant's ears'), cactus-like *Euphorbia ingens* and *Agave attenuata*, and the spiky crowns of *Yucca rostrata*. The serrated leaves and greyish colour of *Melianthus major* play off the foliage of various euphorbia species, including *E. dendroides* and *E. tirucalli*. At a lower level, a wide range of succulents and bromeliads, including six species of aloe, contrast with grasses such as *Muhlenbergia rigens*, the mounded forms of sage (*Salvia canariensis*, *S. chamaedryoides* and *S. pomifera*), the sea lavender *Limonium perezii* and cistus. Plant rarities include *Hymenolepis parviflora* from South Africa, with yellow flower heads and feathery foliage, while the evening garden is perfumed with the scent of the night-blooming jasmine, *Cestrum nocturnum*.

The transition between the two garden spaces has been handled in traditional manner, by means of a tiled pavilion. The contrast when emerging into the larger Islamic Garden is dramatic, as the space opens up to reveal a traditional gridded orchard of citrus trees on a cruciform plan. As the ground surface changes from pink brick to emerald green tiles, it feels like walking into the sea.

A fourfold garden was recreated around a central fountain, each quarter with its own smaller fountain fed by rills, with the walkways edged by clipped rosemary hedges. A tower looks down over the garden from the northwest corner, while dignified pavilions mark the eastern and western ends of the central rill. As Tom points out, this is a style of garden which has remained almost unaltered in Morocco since at least the 11th century: 'The most interesting thing about it is that it is a religious garden, which requires a total suppression of ego. There's nothing about me in there at all.'

The selection and spacing of the fruit trees is based on the 12th-century design of the royal gardens of the Agdal in Marrakech: outer rows of olive enclose the grid of citrus trees, along with date palms. Pomegranates and argans (cultivated for nuts) are grown at the edges. This relaxation of structural formality is common in traditional Moroccan gardens.

The only area of significant departure from historical precedent is in the use of herbaceous planting beneath the trees – the grass *Stipa tenuissima*, native Moroccan lavender and tulbaghias. The plant mix is intended to be an evocation of the Persian idea of the *bustan*, or scented orchard garden.

There is no clear distinction, traditionally, between indoors and outdoors in a riad: most of the pavilions and buildings which surrounded a courtyard were left open-sided and windowless to admit breezes in the warmer months. The coolness and tranquillity offered by the water-refreshed garden still provides a remarkable contrast with the heat and noise of the souk, just a few metres away, over the high wall.

Previous pages
The prickly pear *Opuntia robusta* is a dominant plant in the Exotic Garden, here with the bright yellow feathery leaved *Hymenolepis parviflora*, the spikes of *Aloe vera* and the purple-flowered *Limonium perezii*.

Opposite
A rosemary hedge next to the rill in the Islamic Garden divides the pathway from the olives and stipa grasses.

Right
The meadow-like carpet of grass and lavender, growing below orchard trees, evokes the traditional idea of the *bustan*, or fragrant orchard, in Islamic gardens.

MOUNT ST JOHN

MOUNT ST JOHN

Previous pages
One half of the garden at Mount St John. The yellow tones of phlomis, digitalis and eremurus dominate the upper level, while below the pool the planting becomes darker and richer.

Above
An overview of the estate, showing the Georgian house at centre left, the new modernist extension to its right and the twin gardens below. The valley garden is at lower left.

Opposite
The pool at the halfway point of the terraces, with *Echinacea paradoxa*, *E. pallida* and purple salvia in the foreground, and crimson *Persicaria amplexicaulis* 'Taurus' beyond the acid-green tones of *Euphorbia cornigera*.

This designer's penchant for dramatic contrast is perhaps nowhere more clearly expressed than in this project, in North Yorkshire. It consists of two gardens realized in completely different styles, which are placed next to each other. In fact there are a number of other elements to the overall design, notably an immaculate walled garden and an ambitious valley garden – but the focus here is on the terraced areas on steep ground directly below the house.

The small Palladian mansion of 1720 stands on the site of a Knights Hospitaller priory first recorded in 1017, with panoramic views across rolling countryside towards the Vale of York. Directly in front of the house, Tom has designed a flower garden in two terraced sections, with lawned areas at the centre, an arrangement arising from the client's requirement for two large lawns for marquees for entertaining and fund-raising.

The upper part is in more 'traditional' mode, with a dark and purplish colour scheme, though the plants used would seem to belie this concept: large perennials such as thalictrums, veronicastrums, miscanthus, sanguisorbas and vernonias. Popular among contemporary naturalistic designers, these plants are typically seen at the back of the border. Lower down are echinaceas, heleniums and sedums, mingling with a more traditional palette of masses of geraniums in a range of varieties, as well as 'cottage' flowers such as astrantias. The plants are not deployed in drifts but arranged more in clumps, which gives rise to the slightly more traditional look. Lain across this planting is a wash of alliums earlier in the season, followed by *Verbascum lychnitis* as a rhythmic accent.

Left
Gunnera manicata and *Iris sibirica* planted around the restored fish ponds, which form the central feature of the wild garden in the valley at Mount St John.

Opposite
A quartet of *Crataegus* (thorn) trees around a sculptural fountain in sandstone by Andrew Ewing, on the top terrace.

'I wanted to do something comparatively bold here, in terms of volume and in making quite a strong statement,' Tom says, 'but also something that was fairly recessive – because I thought that if there was too much going on, it would detract from the amazing view.'

The lower flower garden, reached by an elegant flight of new sandstone steps, continues the theme, with the addition of more romantic staples of the classic English garden, such as delphiniums (pale mauve 'Gillian Dallas'), romneya, penstemons, nepeta and peonies. Regale lilies are at the heart of Tom's 'float' planting here, along with the delicate bulbous perennial *Galtonia candicans* used as a filler. At the foot of the lower garden is a ha-ha with a terrace walk above.

A wall and a tall yew hedge divide this part of the garden from the second, more contemporary element, a terraced garden placed directly below a large new wing realized in a recessive (and sympathetic) modernist style next to the older house. This garden is more immediately recognizable as Tom's work, with two large zones of apparently continuous perennial planting of rhythmic character, divided halfway down by an elegant long rectangular pool, with associated deck.

Rough-faced sandstone walls with sawn copings have been deployed to create the retaining walls of the terraces, but otherwise there is little structural interruption other than that provided by the plants themselves. The planting beds effectively overlap and no serious effort is made to keep the 'paths' clear.

The upper terrace here contains more decorative, delicate plant material, with *Phlomis russeliana* (probably the main link plant), *Echinacea tennesseensis* 'Rocky Top' and *Rudbeckia maxima* providing the basis, with coreopsis, salvias, kniphofias and eremurus bubbling up between. A limited number of grasses such as *Stipa calamagrostis* and *Miscanthus sinensis* 'Malepartus' act as a foil to the flowers in late summer, and as a backdrop to seedheads and stems in winter. The sulphurous yellow-green of the odd *Euphorbia seguieriana* creates an even more dramatic contrast.

The zone below the pool has quite a different texture, being made up of mainly bulkier plants in darker hues: veronicastrums, persicarias, eupatoriums and filipendulas, as well as larger clumps of rudbeckias, echinaceas and bright purple *Monarda* 'Scorpion'. With no visible breaks in the planting, the design presents a rich and complex tapestry. At the top of the terraces, the plants are a mix of clipped box balls with *Knautia macedonica*, eryngiums, alliums, purple sedums and blue salvias (mainly varieties of *Salvia* x *sylvestris* including 'Mainacht' and 'Blauhugel').

'Yes, I think it has moments of being indigestible,' reflects Tom, 'but so what? I don't mind a certain amount of apparent chaos, when you might think, "Where am I? How am I going to get out of this place?" But then there will be moments of arresting clarity – like the topiaries at the foot of the terrace.' Tom is referring to a uniform arrangement of identical yew topiaries to one side of the lower planting zone. He calls these shapes 'tumps' – as in, halfway between a tower and a hump.

'I have a bit of an obsession with these topiaries,' he reveals. 'They tend to echo the shapes of trees in the landscape and are also slightly anthropomorphic. They are more interesting than a spire form, which is more of an architectural signifier. I like these things which occupy slightly ambiguous ground between the artificial and the natural, so that you have different levels of apparent naturalness overlaid on each other. You always have to chop down the grasses and things like veronicastrums at the end of the year; I like the idea of something persisting well beyond that.'

Another important structural element is the use of diagonal emphases, partly created by means of the large box balls which are dotted across the space. This picks up on the way the topography of the fields beyond the ha-ha at the bottom of the garden undulates from side to side in a pleasingly disordered manner, naturally animating the foreground.

Overall, this project constitutes planting on a large scale: both terraces together cover almost 1.2 hectares (3 acres), with around 32,000 perennial plants used in the first season. As Tom reflects, 'I am much more drawn to planting on big expanses because you are able to achieve something that is much more multi-dimensional and far less sequential.'

Previous pages
The topmost terrace acts as a prelude, with lower plantings of sedum and *Carex testacea* gathered around flattened box balls.

Left
Terraced lawns fall away from the main house, surrounded by borders conceived in slightly more conservative style. On a clear day, York Minster is visible on the horizon, 40 kilometres (25 miles) to the south.

ATTACHMENT, SEPARATION AND LOSS: A GARDEN NARRATIVE

Tom Stuart-Smith

I have come with my wife Sue to see Villa Farnese at Caprarola in Lazio, Italy. The last time I came, and the time before that, my enquiries were greeted with the reply 'Il casino è chiuso'. But the signora on the phone promised that it is open today. The casino (a summerhouse), and its surrounding garden were created from the mid-16th century by Giacomo del Duca for Cardinal Farnese. It is one of the jewels of Lazio's many gardens and is hidden away some 400 metres (435 yards) from the grand palazzo which dominates the whole town of Caprarola.

   The palazzo, which began life as a fortress, is a tremendous bruiser of a building, built on a pentagonal plan by the architect Vignola. We feel very small as we traverse the brick-paved courtyard and eventually find our way into the most intimidating entrance hall, where three women are chatting behind a desk. It soon transpires that the casino is shut again; shut, not for any particular reason and certainly not one that is advertised anywhere, but shut nonetheless. Downcast but not entirely surprised, we mooch about rather disconsolately, trying to drum up some interest in the magnificent, faded frescoes, and then discover that the other great attraction of the place, the circular courtyard, with the Scala Regia, a stairway so broad that one could ride a horse up it, is shut as well. Time for a long, consoling lunch. But then Sue, who has wandered off to look at some ceiling covered in expanses of Herculean flesh, returns in a state of great excitement. A door out of one of the small rooms on the piano nobile has been left open, and over the sunken moat a little rusting iron bridge leads to freedom. While the attendant's back is turned we sneak out. Hurrying through the neglected terrace gardens laid out by Vignola that face on to two sides of the palace and up a long ramp that leads away into the woods, we are soon in a large park with groves of resinous pine and cedar, densely pungent in the summer heat. It is possible that nobody would really care that we are here, but we duck and hide as if we might be shut up for months in the local prison should we be caught, and this adds a delectable frisson to the quest for the *giardino segreto*, the secret garden.

   We wander now a little aimlessly, and just as we are beginning to despair of our natural garden-finding antennae, and even wondering whether lunch wouldn't have been a better idea after all, there is a telling glimpse of creamy travertine in the distance and I know this must be the entrance to the garden. We arrive at a round marble fountain basin, flanked by heavy rusticated stone walls. The basin is empty and encrusted with dirt, but from here the first magical sequence of the secret garden is revealed. The basin is set at the bottom of a long ramp bisected by a stylized water cascade, with grotesquely carved fish forming the undulating lip.

At the top of the cascade are two giant sculptures of river gods resting on another large basin, from which the cascade appears to emanate, while above this rises the triple-arched facade of the casino, which almost seems to be resting on top of the whole stony, watery ensemble (though of course there is no water today). The effect is intensely theatrical; the scale is intimate, even oppressive, made more so by the heaviness of the sculptural decoration. From here, curving steps then divide around a small courtyard and lead up to the wide, open parterre in front of the casino.

We have arrived and can breathe at last. There is no security guard and no CCTV. But we are overlooked in another, more mysterious way, for we are almost entirely surrounded by twenty-eight tall, stone herms along the balustrade which encloses the garden. The satyric ensemble gives a sense of this being an enchanted clearing, quite apart from reality. The figures each support a tall vase on their heads, which once would have overflowed with flowers. They look on our trespassing with complete indifference, as though there were something much more diverting going on, a spectacle suspended by our uninvited arrival.

The secret garden is one of the most dream-like ideas in the garden repertoire. At Caprarola, it involves a journey from the villa, representing daily reality, through disorientating space into a separate world, where it seems that the norms and constraints of ordinary life do not quite apply. The experience is heightened by extremities of scale and by an iconographic progression from the Herculean heroics of the palace to the enchanted woodland clearing that surrounds the casino. But despite all the magnificence and trappings of antiquity, the principal progression is from the familiar and domestic, albeit palatial, to the remote and fantastic, and it is just a grander, more formalized version of what we potentially experience every time we walk out of the door into our own, more modest garden; we become immersed in its separate life and transported to a parallel world.

This dream-like quality of separateness is one of the most potent characteristics of many great gardens, illusive and unforgettable. In the world of our imagination a garden can represent some prelapsarian state of untroubled bliss and virtue. It is a refuge where worldly cares do not yet exist or can be forgotten. It is an alluring dream which appeals to our belief that in our core there is a pure, unguarded spirit that in the setting of a garden finds its natural habitat.

But for many people, like myself, who are active gardeners, the garden remains a place that, although it provides blissful moments, is less about endless, floaty reverie and more about grappling with a patch of soil – coaxing, tending and never quite being satisfied. Indeed, as a gardener I think that much of the existential grist to gardening is contained in that gap, which so often seems unbridgeable, between the dream and reality. It is a spur to our efforts.

For the gardener, Eden must have been very beautiful but rather boring; too permanent a paradise. I think perhaps that Adam and Eve got themselves thrown out of the garden because there simply wasn't much to do there. God was doing all the gardening. The irony is that once expelled from this garden of infantile bliss, some of us spend the rest of our lives

The parterre in front of the Casino at Caprarola, with surrounding stone herms.

seeking a return, for only when we have lost that state of beloved, cared-for innocence and spend our days working, striving, caring and caught up in the whirl of existence, can we appreciate what is lost. Conversely, to be stuck in the garden of Eden without ever having seen what is beyond its walls is a life half lived.

In *The Portrait of a Lady* Henry James describes the inner garden of his heroine Isabel Archer in a similar vein:

> Her nature had, in her conceit, a certain garden-like quality, a suggestion of perfume and murmuring boughs, shady bowers and lengthening vistas, which made her feel that introspection was, after all, an exercise in the open air, and that a visit to the recesses of one's spirit was harmless when one returned from it with a lapful of roses.

This metaphor of the imagined inner garden is as enchanting as it is improbable. To envisage our own psyche as some delectable, self-sustaining and rose-filled Elysium takes quite a lot of doing, and James here perhaps implies that Isabel is deluding herself if she thinks she can exist in this perfumed isolation.

A different type of enclosed garden metaphor pervades Giorgio Bassani's entire novel, *The Garden of the Finzi-Continis*. This belongs to a rich Jewish family in fascist Italy just before the outbreak of the Second World War. Bassani's description of the garden draws heavily on Ninfa, near Rome, often described as being one of the most romantic gardens in the world, created within the ruins of a medieval fortified town. But crucially, he removes the garden from the southern Lazio countryside to the centre of Ferrara, so there is an increased drama of contrast between the tightly planned, bustling city and the overgrown emptiness of the garden. The hermetically enclosed park in the heart of the city is both a metaphor for the unattainable and enigmatic Micol, much beloved of the narrator, and also of the growing isolation of the family as fascism tightens its grip. They live almost entirely within the separate, timeless world of the garden behind high encircling walls, ignoring the gathering storm that will soon consume them. The lesson of the metaphor is perhaps that the garden cannot be entirely enclosed if it is to have a life; it must have a window open to the world.

Of course, it is rare for a garden to be entirely separate. Most gardens mediate between states of separation and connection with the outside world and with the home, creating a dialogue between the internal and the external, between the private and the public.

The development of my own garden over the last twenty-five years has been something of an extended negotiation of this sort, between a private, rather secret domain and the world outside. We began by carving space out of a 20-hectare (50-acre) wheat field where there was not a single tree or bush, so our principal objective initially was to create a nest-like shelter for our young family, some sort of protection against the flat horizon and the wind. Gradually hedges grew and became like an elaborate filter between us and the surrounding landscape. After ten years of growth, the garden was almost completely enclosed from the landscape, but in a few defined places it maintained a very immediate connection. Stepping into the garden from the house was no longer a leap into the void as it had been before, but began to feel like arriving in a separate territory, with its own pulse and character.

With another passing decade the garden developed a more complex internal structure and a secret, enclosed quality as the skin around it formed. And as this secrecy has evolved, it seems that the garden is increasingly defined by how it meets the surrounding landscape. The garden is made up of a series of semi-enclosed spaces informally planted, and two enclosed spaces that are empty green rooms. Two axes cross and reach out beyond meadows to broad views over the surrounding country. Both axes make the connection between the close, nurtured space and the horizon of forest and sky; they mark a progression from enclosure and refuge to landscape and prospect.

The relationship between the enclosed garden and the wider landscape is something I have been able to explore in a number of different ways in very different gardens. At Woodperry, in Oxfordshire, the enclosed, quartered walled garden is mid-18th century in origin – its layout is a direct descendant of the Persian paradise garden and is perhaps as close as it is possible to get to a garden as an ordered, introspective jewel case. This is not some self-maintaining Eden, however, but an intensely husbanded space, cultivated and artificial, filled with topiary, carefully trained fruit and all sorts of exotic flowers. There is nothing self-sustaining about this; it is clearly a lot of hard work and the outside world is never excluded altogether. The introspection of the garden is set in the wider context of a place open to panoramic views of the Vale of Otmoor, a contrast which endows the setting with an intense drama. It isn't a sealed off box, but sustains a dialogue with the surrounding landscape.

The more I have thought about gardens and their relationships to the surrounding landscape the more I see the constant referencing between garden and setting in terms of a conversation between the internal and the external, like the negotiations we make in a complex social context – between ourselves, our friends and the wider world. The garden becomes a shifting metaphor for the individual in society, being less a walled-off fortress and more a space permeable to influence. And in all its illusive suggestiveness and spatial ambiguity there is an illuminating similarity between the garden and the emotional territory of us as individuals, with the constant fluctuation between connection and separateness that is the stuff of our social discourse. I strive to cultivate my own patch but in doing so sometimes feel that this is at the expense of the view out. I forget to maintain the hedge and can no longer see the surrounding landscape. Gardening becomes an endless balancing act between content and connection.

English gardens share with many of the older gardens of Italy a hierarchical progression from the home to the wilderness, from the familiar and ordered to the distant and wild. From our modern perspective this progression from the familiar enclosure to the wild expanse can be seen to parallel our own emotional ontogeny – from attachment (to the mother) through separation and then, as delineated by the psychoanalyst John Bowlby, to loss. Each time we walk from the hearth to the heath we rehearse the trajectory of our life a little in the same way as the child plays with the idea of a future independence and separation with every game of peekaboo.

In the first book of his trilogy *Attachment and Loss* Bowlby describes the behaviour of young children playing in a park: 'Not infrequently a child of one or two years in a familiar situation is content for half an hour or more to play and to explore using his stationary mother as a base. In maintaining proximity in such situations he relies on orienting towards her, keeping her whereabouts in mind.' In contrast, as soon as the mother tries to move, the child is seized by anxiety and will try to prevent her from doing so. The defined and rooted nature of the home becomes a substitute for the mother figure in our lives, and when we wander to the bottom of the garden and look out over the surrounding fields or rooftops and then return to the house we are just like the two-year-olds in Bowlby's playground.

At my home, as I wander through the crowded spaces close to the house, through the empty rooms beyond and to the view of the surrounding open country, I have this sensation that the layout represents some kind of recapitulation of a life story, that of my family and my own, even though they are, of course, not yet complete. Both in its culture and in its underlying plan, the garden navigates a path from attachment through separation to loss; from containment and connection to the home

Design drawing for the walled garden at Woodperry. It is sunk below the lawn in front of the house and entirely invisible from it.

in the defined and closely planted places close to the house, through reflection, in the green rooms on the edge of the garden, to exposure and some kind of ending in the open views of the surrounding farmland, woodland and horizon.

No garden that I know of illustrates this dialogue between the interior and exterior landscape, whether real or psychological, better than Rousham, in Oxfordshire, created by Charles Bridgeman and William Kent in the early 18th century and my favourite garden in England. Its plan is something I would like to pick up, or to be more accurate, to prise the outline of the garden off the page like a transfer. It shows a square block comprising the house and a grand bowling green connected by a narrow neck to a more irregularly shaped garden sloping down to the River Cherwell. The composition is precisely defined by wall, water or thick yew hedge for its complete extent, except for a small iron fence and gate which runs for about 3 metres (10 feet) between the west front of the house and the ha-ha, where the visitor now enters the garden. Because of its setting along a steep bank on a bend in the river, the garden repeatedly addresses the landscape beyond its limits from different angles, through the organizing prism of the garden foreground and the distancing device of the water, which often lies between the viewer and the view. Beyond the river lies a condensed and idealized portrait of rural England: longhorn cattle, a gothic folly, sporadic traffic on the B4030 and occasional trains hurrying on to Banbury. Being on the other side of the river means that the scenery is close but separate: there is a constant alternation between looking in and looking out. But parallel to this is an equally compelling and recurrent contrast in mood between the erotically charged narrative of the shrubbery and the more forbidding character of the open and formal parts of the garden closer to the house; the deeper the recess, the stronger the suggestion, the sculpture accentuating the difference in mood between the Bacchic internal landscape and the rhetorical, public domain.

It is a garden that lives on and grows in the imagination. Perhaps these seemingly contradictory qualities of suggestiveness and definition, so vividly displayed at Rousham, can be seen as essential requirements for the imaginative cogency of a garden.

The statue known as Apollo within the lower garden at Rousham; almost always approached from the rear.

By this I mean the idea of the garden having a parallel life in the imagination as a virtual space that can be explored, reflected on and discovered almost as much as it is in reality. For every hour spent wandering around Rousham there are hours more to be had wandering about the Rousham-esque recesses of one's mind, like a latter-day, less deluded Isabel Archer.

On one visit on a misty winter's evening, the remains of snow were spread about and the garden seemed more mysterious than ever before. I noticed for the first time that to get into the garden, through that gate between the house and the ha-ha, you have to leave the gravelled drive and walk across a short stretch of turf, as if the connection between the formal area in front of the house and the garden entrance was really quite incidental. There is no instruction. You even have to commit a small transgression to get into the garden in the first place. It becomes separate and illicit, a formalized version of our raid on Caprarola.

The bowling green had become an abstract canvas of snow and grass, exposed by the boots and sledges of the day's visitors, and the lower part of the garden was so deeply enshrouded in freezing fog that stepping from the grand level lawn around the house felt like a descent from the real world of fact and reason to a place where things are only half seen and partly revealed by shifting mists and melting snow; a world of dreams and darkness. The grottoes in Venus' Vale seemed as if they might once have been far more substantial structures, buried by an accumulation of soil and snow over time so that eventually they will become entirely submerged. Never have I seen the place more cryptic and magical.

It is an intensely psychological landscape and one that provokes as many different emotional responses as there are individual visitors. This is in part because, to our modern understanding, the messages of the garden seem somewhat opaque and are in any event slightly eroded by time, but also because it is very easy to get lost. The garden is constructed as a series of quite loosely articulated tableaux. The set pieces themselves may be strongly and even symmetrically constructed – as, for example, Venus' Vale, with its balancing sculpture and central ensemble of descending pools all presided over by the goddess. But the connections between these spaces seem like tangled strings connecting different parts of a mobile, so that even if the garden is visited on a number of occasions it is quite easy to get a little confused. The landscape architect Hal Moggridge once calculated that there are over 1,000 different ways around the garden without re-tracing one's footsteps. I feel sure it is more than this, and it means that it is quite possible

– or even inevitable – that a different route might be taken on each visit. This is part of the plurality of the place. There is a sense that even though the parameters of the territory are rigorously defined, our own experience is unique and very different each time. We each have our own way around the garden.

But whatever route is taken through the garden, the final scene is a view over the River Cherwell to the other world beyond. Perhaps this dialogue between the inner and outer landscape is something William Kent learnt from his time in Italy: an appreciation of the otherness of landscape when seen from within the frame of the garden.

The river that curls silently along the northern edge of the garden at Rousham eventually joins the River Thames at Oxford, but if one were to follow it upstream towards its source and take a small left turn down Sor Brook just south of Banbury, one would, after a few miles of muddy wading, be able to see the site of the first large garden I made, set up on the south-facing side of the valley.

When I began work on the design of a new walled garden at Broughton Grange in 2000 I was acutely conscious that Rousham was just 25 kilometres (15 miles) downstream. While this new garden could not be more different from its riparian neighbour in almost every respect, there are aspects of its relationship with the landscape that were informed and inspired by wandering around Rousham's shady groves.

My client's brief was to make an enclosed walled garden in the middle of an empty field, about 200 metres (650 feet) from the house and with no obvious connection to it. The resulting garden is a square box with an unusually independent quality, a little like an aircraft carrier parked in a field. It is not part of a conventional hierarchical progression from house to horizon.

The plan comprises three terraces that step down the slope. Instead of being entirely enclosed like most walled gardens it is partially open to the countryside on two sides, south and east, whereas the other two sides, north and west, are walled. Without the various visual connections to the surrounding landscape that the open arrangement makes possible, the garden would lose much of its quality, since the essence of the design is about how this square of ground is related to or separate from the fields and woods that surround it, and to what extent it is independent, with its own internal organization and self-sufficiency. This might be thought of in the same way that a writer seeks to describe a character both by their physical qualities and also by the web of interactions that make up being an

The Garden of the Running Footman, St Paul's Walden Bury.

individual – the character's own view of themselves, the author's view, and that of other characters.

If you were to read the garden at Broughton Grange like a book, you would say it has a strong focus, an ordered hierarchy and progression, together with an intense amount of detail, so that at times you are entirely absorbed in the internal workings of this individual plot, but the overall structure is designed as a recipient of the landscape that surrounds it. You are perhaps lost for a moment, immersed in plants, but then you suddenly become aware of a view through trees to the Cherwell valley. The main structural plants in the garden – box, yew and beech – are found commonly in the plantations and hedgerows around the garden, but the detailed planting is entirely exotic. On one open side of the garden are two tall beech tunnels, one on the top terrace and one on the bottom, but in the middle you find yourself right on the edge of the garden, almost tipped over into the field. There is a constant alternation between enclosure and exposure, the exotic and familiar, between connection with and separation from context. This forms the underlying psychological pattern of the garden.

In its separateness, Broughton Grange is in another respect a little reminiscent of the casino garden at Caprarola. The journey from house to garden is an act of separation and discovery, and the sense of the place being a defined territory with a clearly articulated relationship with the outside world is heightened by the fact that it is not a mere appendage. It is, as it were, an adolescent garden, sufficiently independent to have its own organization and relationship to its context, but still tenuously connected to the parent.

When I was an adolescent myself, still happily attached to parents and home, I used to fantasize about making a secret garden in the depths of a wood not far from the house. Surrounded by high beeches and oaks, it was to be a remote, enchanted glade, strewn with violets, ferns and bugle. My idea was that it would be encountered by surprise when out walking and would seem somehow inexplicable. I only got as far as a bit of bramble clearance and transplanting a bucket of primroses, but it continued vividly as a garden in my mind. Later, I was introduced to something like this in reality. A garden so secluded that you might not find it at all. On seeing it for the first time I felt almost a sense of déjà vu, but only later did I connect the imaginary garden I held in my mind with this most sylvan of secret gardens.

By the early 1980s the great landscape architect Sir Geoffrey Jellicoe had already been advising the Bowes-Lyon family on the garden at St Paul's Walden Bury for almost fifty years, and I met him as he made one of his annual visits. The house was a childhood home of Elizabeth Bowes-Lyon, later to become Queen to George VI and then Queen Mother, and I imagine that she would have explored the place as a child oblivious to the fact that this was one of the finest surviving domestic formal gardens of early 18th-century England.

The main garden lies to the east of the house. It begins as a rhetorical square of lawn flanked by pleached lime walks. From this commanding platform, three hedge-lined allées dive into the mysteries of the wood, forming a goosefoot pattern. The broad central ride ends in a stout figure of Hercules, the narrower, northern and most shady allée finishes in a barely perceptible figure of Diana the huntress, and the southern route stretches out of the wood, across the fields, to the tower of the parish church half a mile distant.

The pleasures of striding up and down these woodland rides, however delectably embowered with honeysuckle, do wear thin after a while, and on reaching Diana in her shady bower, enthusiasm begins to wane. But then, along a cross-allée that joins the toes of the goosefoot, another sculpture can be spied quite far off, and there is a suggestion of something a little different in the middle distance – the light bathing the rich, green grass of an open glade.

It is quite possible to walk around the garden for several hours and miss this secret space recast in the 1930s by Geoffrey Jellicoe and known by him as the Garden of the Running Footman. It has the plan of a simple baroque church, sculpted into grass terraces, with a small rotunda on a mound at one end and at the other a formal pond and a copy of a Greek statue of a warrior from which the garden takes its colloquial name. It is almost entirely enclosed and is the archetypal sylvan glade, not quite like the one I dreamed of making, but formalized into an ideal. In spring the turf is thick with cowslips and bugle. It is a quietly theatrical space where you cannot help but feel that you have interrupted some rite of nature that was suspended just the moment before you arrived.

Once, having not been to the garden for some time, I went on my own in early June and stumbled upon it more by luck than judgment. There was a dense quietness and an enthralling moment when I came upon it and the gear of time seemed to slip for a second. The turf was thickly speckled with common spotted orchids and a woodpecker flew quickly into the trees; a place with a life of its own. Returning a year later in the hope of recapturing something of this moment, the orchids had moved on to another part of the garden, like some fugitive spirit.

The Garden of the Running Footman at St Paul's Walden Bury has that distinct quality of separateness which makes us as visitors feel we are in some way secondary to the pulse of the place itself. The balance between humans and our natural environment is very much tipped in favour of nature, so the garden is not just a convenient and decorated outdoor sitting room, subservient to our every wish, but seems to have an independent life. Our position in the scheme of things is re-addressed. We are no longer supreme controllers but observers of a greater process.

It may seem stretching a point to draw any kind of parallel between a garden planned over tens of acres of woodland and a small suburban plot or an average country garden. But even in a small garden it is possible to create some of the sense of connection, journey, separation and independence of spirit that is such a recurrent theme of the gardens I have described. It can be a place where the sense of otherness, of nature and of place is so strong that we have a powerful sense of being. Not as masters of all we survey, but as players in a greater drama.

Whitehall Farm, where I made a garden over a three-year period from 2005, exhibits the sort of restraint without blandness that I'm thinking of. It is on the north Norfolk coast, where a hinterland of beautiful small towns and villages contrasts with vast windswept beaches and empty marshes. In this area near Hunstanton, the villages are built of anything that comes to hand – two types of brick, chalk, carrstone, Hunstanton pink stone (a type of hard pink chalk) and the only really hard material, flint. The rest is sand and mud. The buildings, especially those built with carrstone and chalk, seem, like the landscape, to be in a permanent state of shifting decay, buffeted by the winds off the sea.

Between the marshes and the sea are the dunes, scattered with marram grass and pine trees, crossed by pine boardwalks. It is a landscape where the seasons are marked not only by the alternating growth and dormancy of vegetation, but also by migrations of wildfowl and dramatic tides that flood the marshes twice a day, throwing around all sorts of rubbish, from algae to plastic bottles and rusty metal. It is a landscape of change and impermanence, dissected by reed-filled ditches giving way to glutinous creeks and gulches and then to the sea.

The farm (though it hasn't been a working farm for thirty years) is half a mile from the sea. In making the garden I attempted to draw on the landscape setting by dramatizing the contrast between a refuge, enclosed by walls, hedges and buildings, and what is beyond: the great open skies and north winds. The rich diversity of building materials that dominate the fabric of local farms and villages is not slavishly repeated in the garden, but the extensive use of Corten steel accentuates the colour and texture of the existing brick and tile in a way that few other materials could, yet also defines the garden as a distinct and different place. Similarly, the linear waterways within the garden reflect the pattern of water in the surrounding landscape, but in a highly formalized manner.

The enclosed garden at Whitehall is both an absorption and abstraction of context, and a perceptual device that interprets our relationship with the world beyond the perforated enclosure. There is a vivid contrast between the intellectual, ordered and reflective life as represented by the enclosed garden and the wilder and more uncontrollable world beyond the hedge and wall. The garden within becomes not just a reflection of our relationship with the landscape outside, but a metaphor for ourselves. We are both immersed in the sensual immediacy of the garden and aware of life beyond its limits. Rather than a hermetically sealed Elysium, the garden is a receptacle of influence, part of a dialogue between us and what's out there.

So the garden mediates between two conditions. On the one hand it is a beautiful refuge, while on the other it is a place where a larger drama of landscape, sky and plants, forever on the move, is given focus by garden-making, so that the place becomes more definitely itself. We in the garden are both participants in and spectators of the experience and momentum of place, with its combination of intense energy and concentration in this small area, set in a great open landscape with its inexorable progression from the land to the water.

The sea is an ending; like the apparently un-navigable view of the forest from the edge of my own garden, or the panorama of landscape at Woodperry which we see before descending into the security of the walled enclosure, the sea at Whitehall completes the garden narrative, one which in itself recapitulates our own progression from attachment, through separation, to loss.

View across the flat Norfolk landscape to the sea at Whitehall Farm.

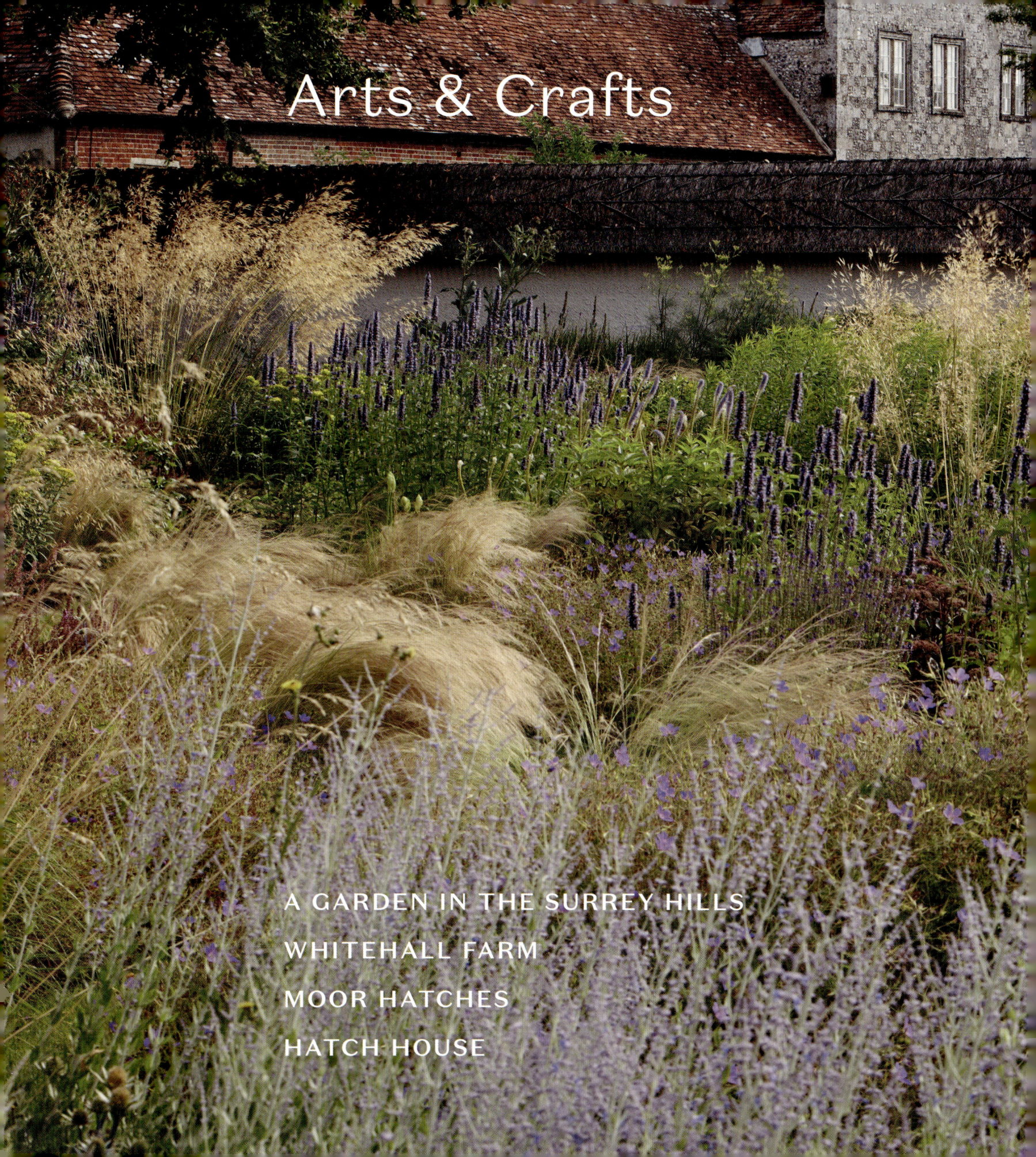

Arts & Crafts

A GARDEN IN THE SURREY HILLS

WHITEHALL FARM

MOOR HATCHES

HATCH HOUSE

A GARDEN IN THE SURREY HILLS

Previous pages
The long border in autumn, with the elegantly drooping seedheads of *Pennisetum alopecuroides* 'Cassian's Choice', tall miscanthus grass and sculptural cardoons.

Above
This detail of a much larger drawing delineates the garden areas near the house. From upper left to lower right: the terraces by the house, the new topiary garden and the sunken pool garden, with the sequoiadendron avenue shooting away above and the converted swimming-pool garden below.

Opposite
The garden made around the old swimming pool, with *Iris pseudacorus* in the foreground.

This Edwardian Arts and Crafts house of 1906 is set in deepest Surrey, not far from Munstead Wood, the home of Gertrude Jekyll, the greatest planting designer of the 20th century. John Coleridge, the architect of the red-brick and half-timbered house of 1906, is not particularly well known, but he was a pupil of Edwin Lutyens and his work here was effective enough, if perhaps a little overdone. The house is dramatically sited on top of a plateau overlooking a sharp slope which falls away on the eastern side. This was originally conceived as a kind of alpine garden, with overtones of what the Edwardians regarded as Japanese (plenty of acers and stone lanterns).

Of more importance to Tom's brief was the fact that two major designers had worked here before him, both in the 1920s. Jekyll herself had laid out a terrace perched above the escarpment, as well as a double herbaceous border and garden 'rooms', and then Percy Cane had extended the terraces and worked on the wider environs of the gardens, adding several summerhouses. As a result, this project is one of the most historically acute to be undertaken by Tom's office.

'This is the most contextual garden I've ever done,' Tom remarks. 'But I just accepted that it is this crazy Arts and Crafts design with a space for every type of garden you can imagine. It was about tying all those threads, all those spaces, together. I wanted to take away the sense that this was a cabinet of curiosities – to make a landscape narrative instead.' Another important aspect to this project was the fact that it was the first one on which Tom collaborated with interior designer Axel Vervoordt, who introduced him to the client. Tom has gone on to work with Vervoordt and his son, Boris, on a number of other commissions.

One of the most intense areas of work for Tom was the series of three terraces on the eastern side of the house, which were completely reworked in an updated Arts and Crafts manner. The top terrace now focuses on a young oak set within tilework, framed by beds against the house containing hydrangeas (*H. petiolaris*, *H. quercifolia*, *H. kawakamii*), clematis (*C.* 'Little Nell', *C. alpina* 'Willy' and 'Frances Rivis', *C. macropetala* 'Lagoon'), clipped box balls, actaeas and epimediums. Roses – *Rosa sanguinea*, *R.* x *odorata* 'Mutabilis' and *R.* 'Buff Beauty' – have been planted against the front balustrade along with santolina and creeping rosemary.

The second terrace is focused on two quartets of figs in pots flanking a circular pool set into the wall, with yew and box balls creating a strong structure for plantings of *Bupleurum fruticosum*, *Centranthus ruber*, *Gaura lindheimeri*, *Verbena bonariensis* and *Euphorbia wallichii*. The third terrace is mainly lavender, before the land falls away dramatically, with the alpine garden descending to a thatched summerhouse with pond. Tom's touch was light in this area – more acers, cornus and the existing Kurume azaleas, overlaid with masses of erigeron and *Campanula* 'Stella' in an effort to harmonize it and reduce complexity. A substantial woodland garden extends down the gradient southeast of the house, where Tom has finessed existing plantings of rhododendrons and magnolias with the likes of *Cornus kousa*, *Stewartia* species and *Cercis canadensis*.

The terrace on the south side of the house looks down a long grass vista flanked by trees. It was reworked in a similar manner as the eastern terraces, the view now framed by a series of large box domes.

The main 'garden rooms' are situated northeast of the house. First is the Topiary Garden (empty when Tom arrived), where the formality of yew topiaries is undercut by a wild-looking meadow of *Pennisetum alopecuroides* 'Cassian's Choice', with digitalis, campanulas, verbascums, *Ammi majus*, *Catananche caerulea* 'Major' and *Euphorbia oblongata*. Next is the Fountain Garden, a sunken garden with a shallow rectangular pool which is perhaps the most purely Arts and Crafts of all the spaces.

Previous pages
Yew shapes in the Topiary Garden created by Tom, with tall *Verbascum bombyciferum* 'Arctic Summer', magenta *Dianthus carthusianorum* and (right) white *Centranthus*.

Left
A wild setting for the tennis court.

Opposite
One of the four corner arbours in the walled garden, each of which is planted with pears.

Previous pages
The sunken garden, one of the original Arts and Crafts elements of the garden, planted with *Hydrangea arborescens* 'Annabelle' and *Rosa rugosa* 'Schneezwerg'.

Opposite
The garden extends to woodland and extensive meadows. Here a birch stands amid *Narcissus* 'Actaea'.

Right
Frothing *Alchemilla mollis* and hydrangeas in the sunken garden, with the tall gables of the house beyond.

The pool is framed by a romantic mix of *Hydrangea arborescens* 'Annabelle' with the creamy white Pemberton shrub rose 'Moonlight', complemented by peonies, lilies, abutilon, romneya, verbascums, orlaya and scores of irises in season.

Just east of and below these 'rooms' is the old swimming pool garden, where an unusual thatched pavilion overlooks what was a kidney-shaped pool that was naturalized by Tom. Now it is surrounded by gunnera, molinia grasses, eupatoriums, valerian, irises, euphorbias, osmanthus, aquilegias, darmera and numerous persicarias, making it into a truly secret spot with glimpses of the house above.

The great double border, the longest Tom has ever designed, lies just beyond the Fountain Garden. Here Tom emphatically departed from Jekyll's original plans (which survive), opting for a border possessed of rhythm and continuity along its entire length, as opposed to an episodic narrative in the Arts and Crafts manner. 'There is both change and continuity in the border,' Tom explains. 'The eremurus go all the way down, for example. The colour scheme is quite unified and you only notice the variations if you look quite closely. I quite often do that.'

West of the double border is the walled garden, which has been radically redesigned as an orchard of crab apples (mainly *Malus* 'Evereste') above a meadow, with a small reflecting pool at the centre. As Tom explains, 'The irony is that in the past the kitchen garden would have been the most crowded part of the garden, and it has become this empty space. I suppose this was a reaction to the inevitable congestion you feel in a garden like this. This is the only area where you get a sense of release from a feeling of enclosure and obsessive detail.' The four corners of the space are occupied by steel arbours with 'Conference' pears trained on them, while the meadow is rich in field scabious, wild carrot and lady's bedstraw.

There is much more to this garden, which extends across more than 4 hectares (10 acres). To the northeast is a large area of meadow planted with specimen trees, which Tom has cleared and replanted so it feels more relaxed and naturalistic. 'A lot of this was about simplification,' Tom concludes. 'It was about limiting the number of transitions between spaces so that when they do happen, they are really powerful.'

WHITEHALL FARM

WHITEHALL FARM

Previous pages
This is a garden of strong form and colour – from materials such as local brick and tiles, and plants including box topiaries, *Miscanthus sinensis* 'Ferner Osten' (right) and the willow *Salix exigua*, interspersed along the wall with fountains of green Cretan hemp, *Datisca cannabina*.

Above
Preparatory drawing showing the farmhouse at left and the ancillary buildings (reconceived by Ptolemy Dean) to its right, and Tom's enclosed garden areas below. At top left is the meadow in front of the sea.

Opposite
There is constant interplay between the garden's structural forms and the architecture of the farm.

'If you look at the photographs of this place when the client bought it, it was pretty unprepossessing,' Tom says. 'The farmhouse was painted white, the garden had no character at all and there was a giant agricultural shed in the middle of it all. There was a vast caravan park next to it and a huge Leyland cypress hedge. It was a really depleted, dispiriting place. What's more there was no connection with the marshland and the sea to the north.'

The architect Ptolemy Dean, a regular collaborator of Tom's, was commissioned to renovate the farm buildings on the site, indicating the potential for a series of enclosed spaces which could stand as individual gardens. 'Ptolemy really unleashed the underlying qualities of the site,' Tom says. The farmhouse itself was small enough in context not to have to act as the focus of the design. That decision enabled Tom to envisage a garden with an extended and elongated feel, stretched out along the different spaces. As a result, Whitehall Farm does not have the appearance of a prettified farm, but rather there is a sense of a place made up of a non-hierarchical sequence of gardens, each of which has its own purpose and integrity.

'Ptolemy transformed what was really quite a motley collection of buildings into a wonderfully vibrant ensemble, where the most is made of the Norfolk melee of building materials,' Tom explains. 'In between and around the buildings we have made a garden that draws on its landscape setting by accentuating the contrast between what is within the civilized domain and what is "out there" – on the edge.' The garden has a low-slung feel to it, as if it functions as a sanctuary of sorts, hunkered down against whatever the elements can throw at it in this exposed coastal zone.

Left
Corten steel panels divide up the garden space and create a foil for the complexity of plant forms and colour.

Opposite
A quiet zone, with multi-stemmed *Rhus typhina* growing amid hakonechloa grass.

    The main garden area, south of the house, is divided in two by a long hedge of clipped beech, while further beech panels are used throughout to subdivide the spaces of the garden. The other recurring material is Corten steel, used for panels and architectural elements such as a pergola, where the distinctive orange-brown tones of the metal complement the local carrstone used for building. 'I do love Corten as a material – in the right place,' Tom reflects. 'There is a nice robustness to it. I think this was the first time I used it and I slightly fell in love with it – so it's pretty full-on here. It was the stimulus for using Corten in my Chelsea Flower Garden for the *Daily Telegraph* in 2006.'

    The Corten steel also subtly engages with the idea of the rural-industrial picturesque – rusting metal is a familiar sight in farmyards and on beaches. Other echoes of the locale can be found in the *Miscanthus* grasses, which bring to mind the reeds of the coastal landscape, while certain plants (such as hemerocallis) pick up the colour of the buildings and Tom's canals reference the sheer wateriness of this marshy area. Tom describes his method within the garden as, 'an abstraction of what lies beyond'.

    The sward directly in front of the house and aligned on its large central gable has been left almost unadorned, except for a line of yew domes and a single walnut tree, since the general strategy throughout was to align the garden areas with the ancillary buildings. The large garden space closest to the house consists of a series of shallow grass 'steps' defined by long horizontal strips of Corten, with a line of flattened box topiary domes running up one side. The garden rises up to a water parterre consisting of three parallel canals, at first invisible because of the spectacular horticultural effusions in the four planting panels which alternate between them. These beds are rhythmically planted with drifts of *Eryngium yuccifolium*, *Vernonia crinita*, *Euphorbia griffithii* 'Dixter', *Alchemilla erythropoda* and varieties of hemerocallis alongside veronicastrums, sanguisorbas,

eupatoriums, carex and molinia grasses. The panels of Corten beyond (uplit at night) serve to emphasize further the underlying contrast in this design between fluidity and solidity.

The adjacent garden area is divided in two: in the half closest to the house a swimming pool garden is complemented by a lawn strewn with box topiaries in a wide range of shapes. Tom wanted the garden as a whole to contain echoes of the random detritus that is thrown up by the sea on to the beach and dunescape, and this scattering of decorous evergreen 'lumps' reflects that. Beyond the pool area and topiary lawn is a small glade of sumach trees (*Rhus typhina*) now underplanted with miscanthus grasses (the original hakonechloa having succumbed to chafer grubs), adjacent to which are vegetable beds, a reminder that Whitehall Farm was formerly a place devoted to food production.

On the northern, sea-facing side of the house, Tom chose to accentuate the natural qualities of the setting, extending two existing ponds which herald the marsh beyond and supplementing the population of pollarded willows. Highland cattle are grazed in the adjoining field, which has been turned over from sugar-beet production to a meadow of cowslips, oxeye daisies, plantains, scabious and buttercups. From here the sea can be heard, a couple of fields away.

There is quite a contrast between this part of the garden and the much more finished and pristine elements elsewhere, and this is deliberate. 'I like accentuating differences,' Tom says. 'I try to make different areas seem more "essential", accentuating contrasts in the process.'

In this case those contrasts narrate a sense of progression from the enclosed gardened space to the open empty fields and dunes beyond, a sensation Tom describes as 'the idea of this being a garden on a threshold of land'.

Previous pages
Corten steel risers create an elegant terraced effect, with clipped box in terracotta pots echoing the colours of building materials.

Opposite
A new pond on the sea side of the house, with purple loosestrife (*Lythrum salicaria*) at the margin.

Right
Pleasingly 'misshapen' box topiaries on the lawn by the swimming pool.

MOOR HATCHES

MOOR HATCHES

Previous pages
The walled swimming pool garden, with its distinctive thatched wall and perennial plantings including, in the foreground, *Phlox paniculata* 'Franz Schubert' and *Echinacea purpurea* 'White Swan'.

Above
The original design drawing which shows the walled garden to the right and the courtyard garden to its left, next to the house. The modernist extension to the house (with sloping roof) was not realized. The River Avon is at the foot of the drawing.

Opposite
The colour and form of *Perovskia* 'Blue Spire' is echoed by *Agastache* 'Blackadder' behind.

This is a garden of three distinct parts, set on the banks of the River Avon in Wiltshire. First, there is a courtyard area in front of the house; then there is a walled garden containing a swimming pool, which is the ornamental heart of the scheme; and finally an open lawn or meadow leads down to the riverbank, with its wilder feeling.

The house, which describes an L-shape and is just one room deep in places, was reconfigured by architect Jonathan Ross, who also created a courtyard in front of it by adding an entrance wing in the brick and knapped flint which is the local vernacular. Tom planted this partly enclosed courtyard (it is open on the river side) in the form of a staggered grid of specimens of crab apple *Malus* 'Evereste' set in planting beds and accessed by stone and gravel paths. This is a good example of the way this designer utilizes classic modernist design tropes – in this case the tree grid, à la Dan Kiley, the American landscape architect – and tweaks them to suit a different situation, here a village idiom. The planting is at the traditional end of the spectrum, in the context of Tom's work, with various roses ('Étoile de Hollande', 'Wilhelm', 'Guinée', *R.* x *odorata* 'Mutabilis' and *R. chinensis* 'Sanguinea'), peonies, six species of euphorbia, sedums and beech hedging.

'I wanted to create something a bit more "husbanded",' Tom explains. 'The crabs give it the feel of a slightly more cultivated, looked-after space than the walled garden. Inevitably, being surrounded by these strongly vernacular buildings, this space has slightly more of a sense of tradition in terms of the materials used.'

Nevertheless, certain elements mark the courtyard out as distinctively Tom's design – plants such as *Sanguisorba officinalis* 'Red Thunder', *Ageratina altissima*

'Chocolate', *Phlomis italica*, *Persicaria amplexicaulis* 'Blackfield', large clumps of *Echinacea purpurea* 'Magnus' and heleniums including 'Moerheim Beauty' and 'Rubinzwerg'. Grasses – *Anemanthele lessoniana*, *Carex testacea*, *Panicum virgatum* 'Hänse Herms' – lend definition to the space into the winter, while scores of vibrant tulips pop up in spring.

The courtyard forms a richly coloured overture, but it is the walled garden, on the other side of the house, which is the horticultural highlight. This large space is bounded on its far side by a remarkable feature: a wall with a V-shaped thatched 'roof', designed by Tom in the local vernacular. The white-rendered wall establishes the spatial order for the design, which is characterized by long, serene horizontals in the form of wooden pathways and a series of rectangular planting beds which artfully conceal the swimming pool at the centre. There is a slight level change across the space which allows the pool to sink a little out of view and create a feeling of enclosure to the pool terrace. A bench, for sunbathing, runs along the whole 20-metre (65-ft) length of one side of the pool. During the development of the design Tom had initially tried to find a marginal place for the pool, but as the client wanted such a large one, he decided to make it central as well as beautiful.

Other new walls were constructed from zinc – the colouring chosen to echo the limestone clunch stone of the fine village house visible in the background, and the chalk cob walls. This, in turn, dictated the muted colour palette of the planting (all the echinaceas and agastaches have been taken out over time). It is structured around groupings of *Nepeta racemosa* 'Walker's Low', salvias in five varieties, cranesbill geraniums, box clumps and beech hedges. Grasses also play an important role here – varieties such as *Miscanthus sinensis* 'Graziella' and 'Cascade', *Sporobolus heterolepis*, *Pennisetum alopecuroides* 'Hammeln' and a number of different panicums and stipas.

'There are pretty strong rules for colour here – there's nothing very bright,' Tom says. 'There is a lot of nepeta, salvia and grasses, but I think it still has a freshness and directness to it. I chose a palette of about twenty plants and just

Left
Rosa x *odorata* 'Mutabilis' and euphorbias among the crab apples which define the entrance courtyard.

Opposite
Salvia, *Stipa tenuissima* and (foreground) *Allium sphaerocephalon* in the walled garden.

Previous pages
The garden in winter, with sedums and grasses resplendent even in their dormant period. For the owners, this is the garden's best moment.

Opposite
The orange-red flowers of *Helenium* 'Moerheim Beauty' play off the acid-green of euphorbia in the entrance courtyard.

Right
Grasses and perennials erupt from a planting bed near the swimming pool.

repeated them, almost like a parterre planting.' Key species include thalictrums (replacements for too rampant cephalaria), eupatoriums, veronicastrums ('Spring Dew' and 'Temptation') and *Verbena hastata* f. *rosea*. A break in the beech hedge on the river side reveals a view into a farmer's field beyond, reminding swimmers of the rural setting. The owners say their favourite moment in the walled garden is January – an unusual sentiment to come across, and testament to the powerful structural basis of the planting regimen.

And then there is the lawn, which describes a gentle gradient to the river's edge. Tom removed a large number of specimen trees (several with red or copper leaves) from this area, leaving only a tulip tree (*Liriodendron*), in order to enhance the naturalistic tone. His idea was for long pasture with mown paths, flanked by wildflower panels. For now, the space is being mostly maintained as a lawn, since this is still essentially a family garden, but the area of wild flowers between the house and the river is being gradually expanded, and will eventually link the two.

A boggy area near the river has been formed into three separate ponds, planted with marginal plants such as irises, rodgersia, gunnera and lythrum. The clients say that one of the principles that they have learnt from Tom is that, 'the further you are from the house, the more you give back to nature'.

HATCH HOUSE

Previous pages
One of the Corten steel water tanks in the front garden, surrounded by hakonechloa and veronicastrums, with purple *Verbena bonariensis* in the background.

Above
On this drawing the farmyard is in the foreground, followed by the front garden and farmhouse. The rear garden creates a connection with the surrounding landscape, with views up to the Downs.

Opposite
Steps in the front garden, with burgeoning verbena behind the hakonechloa and a clipped box hedge.

As well as very large projects, Tom Stuart-Smith's practice has worked on scores of gardens of less than a couple of acres, in addition to townhouse, courtyard and roof gardens. Hatch House is representative of this more modestly scaled strand of work. The property, near Newbury, in Berkshire, is frequently used for shooting weekends, and the garden has been designed to look at its best in the late summer and autumn months. It is also a garden for socializing in, while functioning too as a place of tranquillity and respite. 'The client has given up on big, show-off houses,' Tom says. 'This is more of a retreat. It's somewhere to go and relax and hang out.'

The planting style is so intensified that this garden could almost be described as a concentrated or distilled version of some of Tom's designs for larger acreages (though he never precisely repeats planting plans or layouts). On the north side of the house, especially, the garden feels full of incident, with new vistas and complex plant associations opening up at almost every step. Yet Tom admits that he was not very inspired on his first visit here. 'My heart sank, slightly – it was a dreary place with a horrid little garden and no sense of the landscape at all.' But for Tom, a good working relationship with a client is much more important than any difficulties presented by a site, and Hatch House is one of those projects where the client has turned into a friend. With little opportunity to take advantage of the surrounding landscape, Tom has turned the garden in on itself and made a capsule of intense horticulture, surrounded by play areas (tennis court, football pitch) and an orchard.

The garden on the north (front) side of the house is a small, simple rectangle, yet it contains a number of Tom's signature design motifs: a grid of rectangular

Previous pages
Double-flowered *Anemone* x *hybrida* 'Königin Charlotte' flourishes under a witch hazel in the wilder rear garden.

Opposite
The front garden, with clumps of *Calamagrostis* x *acutiflora* 'Karl Foerster' conspiring to obscure the water tanks in late summer.

Right
A path leading to a small stream in the garden, with the foliage of *Helleborus argutifolius* and *Euphorbia characias* subsp. *wulfenii* in the foreground.

planting beds, narrow Corten steel water tanks, clipped evergreen shapes and small trees used to create a subtle sense of structure. A typical planting bed will contain a mix of bulkier subjects such as *Veronicastrum virginicum* 'Fascination' and *Euphorbia martinii* along with drifts of *Echinacea purpurea* 'Magnus', *Amsonia tabernaemontana* var. *salicifolia* and grasses – *Panicum virgatum* 'Shenandoah' and *Calamagrostis* x *acutiflora* 'Karl Foerster'. The delicate *Astrantia major* 'Claret' is used at the fronts of the beds and also mingles with hakonechloa grass along the east side of the garden, under a cloud-pruned box hedge. On the west side, another cloud hedge is fronted by more *P. virgatum* 'Shenandoah' and swathes of irises in spring. Several surprises are tossed into the overall plant mix, such as thistle-like *Centaurea* Phoenix hybrids and spiky purple-silver *Eryngium bourgatii*.

The Corten steel water tanks add an unexpected note of formality and composure amid the horticultural exuberance. 'This garden brings the modern and vernacular really scratching together,' Tom says. 'The contemporary can be found in the textured paving, the Corten steel and all this cloudy hedging; the vernacular is in the brick walls, the Herefordshire sandstone cobbles and the reclaimed York stone, selected for its warm colouring. It's quite an intense little space.'

The rear garden, sloping to the south, has a looser feel, with a small terrace by the house (*Skimmia* x *confusa* 'Kew Green', thymes, rosemary) giving way to a series of eight squarish beds planted as wildflower meadow – campion, bird's-foot trefoil, oxeye daisies, scabious, greater and lesser knapweed, wild carrot, red and white clover, lady's bedstraw and meadow cranesbill. Height and structure is provided by an informal planting of crab apples (*Malus* 'Evereste' and 'Donald Wyman'). In addition, there are yew topiaries running down the west side of the garden. These are left to grow 'fuzzy', as the head gardener puts it, and clipped only once, in spring.

Finally, the house itself is festooned in climbing plants including clematis, trachelospermum and especially roses, in old-fashioned varieties such as 'Étoile de Hollande', 'Francis E. Lester', 'Malvern Hills', 'Blush Noisette' and 'Albertine'. This is Tom working in his most romantic, most 'English' register.

The ungardened garden

LA GRANJA ALNARDO

LA GRANJA ALNARDO

Previous pages
Experimental naturalistic horticulture set around a visitor building designed by Henning Larsen at a vineyard in Spain's Duero Valley.

Above
This drawing is unusual in Tom's portfolio in that it was made some time after work had begun on the project, and does not depict an 'end point'. The main planted area is below the building, the swimming pool is to the right, and the trees and shrubs of the existing landscape can be seen on the valley slopes above.

Opposite
Stipa gigantea and santolina on the route to the swimming pool, part of a designed circuit walk of the garden.

This project represents the direction Tom's most recent work is moving in, towards a concept of garden-making that is based more on horticultural experimentation and management of habitat, as opposed to active design intervention resulting in a human 'signature'. It is a strategy which can be seen in the work of a number of contemporary practitioners, and is in some ways a logical development of the 'naturalistic turn' in garden style over the past twenty years. Core tenets include an emphasis on the idea of the replication of plant communities observed in the wild, and a sense that gardening should be more 'sustainable', with less or no irrigation required, and plants left to find their own places in a scheme, rather than being placed there by the 'godlike' designer-creator. The garden-maker is clearly still the prime progenitor of the result (though even that is debatable), but is perhaps more akin to a conductor leading an orchestra, as opposed to a composer writing a score.

On the southern slopes of the valley of the Ribera del Duero in central Spain, 30 kilometres (18 miles) east of Valladolid, a Danish winemaker has built a visitor centre for a vineyard and biodynamic farm. He has worked closely with Tom on the creation of a new kind of garden around the buildings. As Tom comments: 'Nowhere have I felt more strongly that what I am doing as a designer is setting a process in motion – as it were, pushing a boat out into the water.'

In many ways this almost 1-hectare (2-acre) plot is not a 'garden' at all, more an ongoing experiment with a plant community geared to a climate where the long winters can be harsh (-10°C is normal) and the even longer summers punishingly hot and dry (up to 40°C) on the open slopes of the valley. Spring and autumn barely

Left and opposite
Limestone paths and terraces have been left deliberately fragmented at the edges to allow rosemary, santolina, helichrysum and other plants to colonize. A large specimen of the native evergreen oak has been left in situ.

seem to feature. The chalky, rocky soil is unsuitable for conventional gardening and the emphasis here is on native plants, or plants which can behave like natives.

The plot extends around the stone-clad modernist main building, by Danish architect Henning Larsen, and tumbles down the steep and rocky hillside towards the farm, nominally also extending uphill through scrubby maquis towards the ridge of the valley. It is not clear where the garden ends and nature begins, which is all part of the plan. The desire is for the garden to appear to be a continuation and elaboration of the surrounding maquis scrubland. The main garden area is ranged across a wide slope below the visitor building, extending along a terraced walkway towards a pool and small gym building. The native plant community on the open scrubland of these steep valley sides consists of bushy forms of the evergreen oak, *Quercus rotundifolia* and *Q. faginea*, *Juniperus thurifera*, rosemary, santolina and a particularly prickly genista growing on the gypsum-rich material which passes for soil.

For the areas around the building, Tom came up with a matrix planting plan with the rhythmic intensity which is his horticultural signature, dependent on key native plants such as *Santolina chamaecyparissus* and *S. rosmarinifolia*, *Geranium sanguineum*, *Helichrysum italicum*, *Dorycnium pentaphyllum*, *Cistus albidus* and *Euphorbia characias* subsp. *wulfenii*, as well as maquis herbs such as rosemary and hyssop. 'It is accelerated and diversified regeneration,' Tom explains. 'Closer to the building it is very much augmented.'

Rather than conventional planting plans, Tom made colourful plans like Damien Hirst spot paintings to describe the planting pattern to the vineyard workers who were doing the planting. This basic mix has been extended with a wide range of other plants as a supporting cast, many sourced from specialist French nurseryman Olivier Filippi and with his active involvement in the choice. Among the plants from Filippi's stock, which are now performing well, are species of phlomis, thyme, perovskia, salvia, euphorbia and achillea – the last (*A. nobilis*) making a spectacular summer

show. Tom says Filippi's plants fared better than most because he grows plants in soil as opposed to peat-based compost, which lessens the shock when they are planted out. But the challenge – finding plants tolerant of lime, extreme cold and drought – remains considerable. The owner creates a biodynamic preparation which is sprayed on the soil once a year, the only such intervention. The intention is that the landscape is very low maintenance and becomes to a great extent self-sustaining.

Designer and client knew that trial and error would be a decisive factor, and the conditions did indeed prove too much for a disconcertingly large proportion of a 2016 test planting of forty species (ten specimens of each). In the following year, 7,000 plants were laid out in the garden and it was salutary both to see just how many succumbed, and to accept the slow growth of many of those that did survive. Nevertheless, the plants which have thrived – notably achillea, phlomis, rosemary, bupleurum, euphorbia, thymes, *Geranium sanguineum*, anthemis, phillyrea and cistus – have formed a hummocky, shrub-dominated plant community which acts as a visual continuation of the wider landscape. The original planting was oversown with perennial and biennial seed in consultation with 'Pictorial Meadows' designer Nigel Dunnett, and it is from this layer that the achillea and anthemis derived, though Tom anticipates their presence will lessen over time.

As the larger shrubs, including *Euphorbia characias* subsp. *wulfenii* and *Cistus albida*, become established, they are gradually supplanting the achillea as a dominant species. The yellow mounds of *Santolina chamaecyparissus*, offset by purple spikes of *Salvia officinalis* and *Hyssopus officinalis*, form a dense matrix close to the building. The deep green of rosemary forms a counterpoint, while in the background, further up the hillside, small clumps of the erect native grass *Stipa barbata* are just visible.

As Tom observes: 'This is the only project I have done where I have not made a bird's-eye drawing of how it will eventually look.' That is because he and his client do not know quite what the result will be. It's an approach which has been gradually evolving in Tom's work over the years – Vergelegen follows a similar rationale – and we can expect to see it develop further.

Previous pages
The view from the swimming pool to the visitor building. The same limestone, in different forms, has been used across the scheme.

Opposite
Santolina, marjoram, achillea and sage are among the local maquis plants encouraged almost up to the walls of the buildings.

Right
By the entrance drive the planting is dominated by white *Achillea nobilis*, alongside more ephemeral herbs such as *Salvia sclarea* var. *turkestanica* and *Echium vulgare*.

CAREER TIMELINE

THE BARN
Hertfordshire, UK
1986   (see pp. 46–56)

CHELSEA FLOWER SHOW 1998, CHANEL
London, UK
1998

GUIST HALL
Norfolk, UK
1998

CHURCH COURT, INNER TEMPLE
With Ptolemy Dean
London, UK
1998

MANOIR DE LA TRINITÉ
Jersey, UK
1998

MUNDEN HALL: SWIMMING POOL GARDEN
Hertfordshire, UK
1999

BRIZES LODGE
Oxfordshire, UK
2000

BROCKHAMPTON COTTAGES
Herefordshire, UK
2000

BROUGHTON GRANGE
With Ptolemy Dean
Oxfordshire, UK
2000   (see pp. 16–25)

CHELSEA FLOWER SHOW 2000, GARDEN HISTORY SOCIETY AND LAURENT-PERRIER
London, UK
2000

GORHAMBURY
Hertfordshire, UK
2000

HILLET
Condom, Gers, France
2000

KELSO PLACE
London, UK
2000

CHELSEA FLOWER SHOW 2001, LAURENT-PERRIER
With Jamie Fobert
London, UK
2001

THE QUEEN'S JUBILEE GARDEN
WINDSOR CASTLE
Berkshire, UK
2001   (see pp. 130–39)

WOODPERRY HOUSE
Oxfordshire, UK
2001

ARBURY HALL: SWIMMING POOL GARDEN
Warwickshire, UK
2002

BADBURY HILL
Oxfordshire, UK
2002

EASTBACH COURT
With Smallwood Architects
Herefordshire, UK
2002

EASTNOR CASTLE:
REPLANTING ARBORETUM
Herefordshire, UK
2002

FORT BELVEDERE /
WINDSOR GREAT PARK
Surrey, UK
2002   (see pp. 174–84)

GLEBE HOUSE, SOUTHILL
Bedfordshire, UK
2002

LESSOR GRANGE
With Ptolemy Dean
Oxfordshire, UK
2002

LOWER VICAR'S FARM
With Johnston Cave Architects
Buckinghamshire, UK
2002

THE OLD RECTORY, WRAMPLINGHAM
Norfolk, UK
2002

WYCLIFFE HALL
With Ptolemy Dean
County Durham, UK
2002   (see pp. 140–51)

AUBREY HOUSE
With Todd Longstaffe-Gowan
London, UK
2003

HOUSE IN BLOOMFIELD TERRACE
London, UK
2003

BURRISHOOLE LODGE
County Mayo, Ireland
2003

CHELSEA FLOWER SHOW 2003,
LAURENT-PERRIER
London, UK
2003

CLINK WHARF APARTMENT
London, UK
2003

GRENDON COURT
Herefordshire, UK
2003

LECKHAMPTON
Cambridgeshire, UK
2003

OXHILL HILL FARM
Warwickshire, UK
2003

SAGAPONAK GARDEN
New York, USA
2003

TRIPPLETON HOUSE
Herefordshire, UK
2003

UPTON VIVA
Oxfordshire, UK
2003

WATLINGTON PARK
With Smallwood Architects
Oxfordshire, UK
2003

WILBURY PARK
With Peregrine Bryant
Wiltshire, UK
2003

HEVENINGHAM HALL
Suffolk, UK
2004

HOUSE IN LADBROKE GROVE
London, UK
2004

SKER HOUSE
Glamorgan, UK
2004

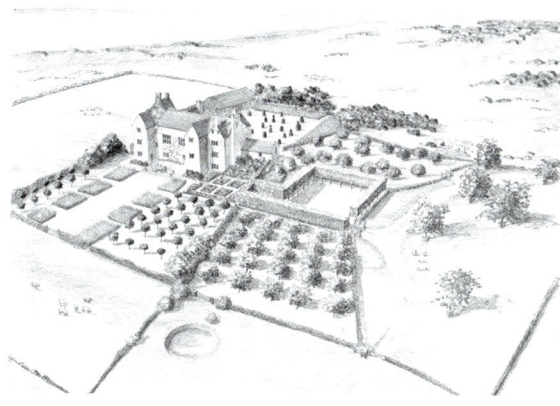

TRENTHAM
With Piet Oudolf
Staffordshire, UK
2005   (see pp. 194–203)

CHARLEVILLE
County Wicklow, Ireland
2005   (see pp. 66–75)

CHELSEA FLOWER SHOW 2005, LAURENT-PERRIER
London, UK
2005

DEANE HOUSE
Basingstoke, UK
2005

HOUSE IN KENSINGTON PALACE GARDENS
London, UK
2005

KITTISFORD HOUSE
Somerset, UK
2005

OAKHILL
Kent, UK
2005   (see pp. 204–11)

WHITEHALL FARM
With Ptolemy Dean
Norfolk, UK
2005   (see pp. 262–71)

CHELSEA FLOWER SHOW 2006, DAILY TELEGRAPH
London, UK
2006

MALVERLEYS
Berkshire, UK
2006

SNOWDENHAM HOUSE
Surrey, UK
2006   (see pp. 26–33)

WORMSLEY
Buckinghamshire, UK
2006

RHS WISLEY: BICENTENARY GARDEN
Surrey, UK
2007   (see pp. 212–21)

COGSHALL GRANGE
Cheshire, UK
2007   (see pp. 110–20)

HILL TOP FARM
Worcestershire, UK
2007

MOOR HATCHES
Wiltshire, UK
2007   (see pp. 272–81)

MOUNT ST JOHN
With Hall and Hoyle Architects
Yorkshire, UK
2007   (see pp. 232–40)

THE DOWER HOUSE, UPTON GREY
Hampshire, UK
2007

HOUSE IN WARWICK SQUARE
With Rose Uniacke and Vincent Van Duysen
London, UK
2007

CAN VINGUT
Ibiza, Spain
2008

CHELSEA FLOWER SHOW 2008, LAURENT-PERRIER
London, UK
2008

HOUSE NEAR HENLEY
Berkshire, UK
2008

LADYRIDGE FARM
Herefordshire, UK
2008

HOUSE IN PEMBRIDGE GARDENS
With Jamie Fobert Architects
London, UK
2008

RHS HARLOW CARR: WOODLAND MASTERPLAN
Yorkshire, UK
2008

HOUSE IN THORNHILL ROAD
With Mark Guard Architects
London, UK
2008

CHISENBURY PRIORY:
FLOWER BORDERS
Wiltshire, UK
2009

CROWE HALL: A WALLED GARDEN
Suffolk, UK
2009

CULHAM COURT
With Woody Clark, Jamie Fobert, Purcell,
Robert Trembath
Berkshire, UK
2009   (see pp. 88–99)

HATCH HOUSE
Berkshire, UK
2009   (see pp. 282–89)

PILTON HOUSE
Rutland, UK
2009

SHIRBURN LODGE
With Mike Rundell Associates
Oxfordshire, UK
2009–20

THE CONNAUGHT HOTEL GARDEN OF ILLUSION
London, UK
2009

VILLA MUMM:
ENTRANCE COURTYARD PLANTING
Frankfurt, Germany
2009

YOTES COURT
With Sergison Bates
Kent, UK
2009   (see pp. 162–73)

CHELSEA FLOWER SHOW 2010,
LAURENT-PERRIER
London, UK
2010

CLARIDGE'S HOTEL: INSTALLATION
London, UK
2010

ENCOMBE
With Mark Deaves
Dorset, UK
2010   (see pp. 76–87)

HOUSE IN PALACE GARDENS TERRACE
London, UK
2010

PINDRUP FARM
With Ptolemy Dean Architects
Gloucestershire, UK
2010

RHS HARLOW CARR: WOODLAND
Yorkshire, UK
2010

HOUSE IN RUE SAINT-JAMES
Paris, France
2010

SHANKS HOUSE
With Ptolemy Dean
Somerset, UK
2010

HOUSE IN TEMPLEWOOD AVENUE
With Tony Fretton
London, UK
2010

VIRGINIA WATER COTTAGE
Berkshire, UK
2010

CASA GALERA
Ibiza, Spain
2011

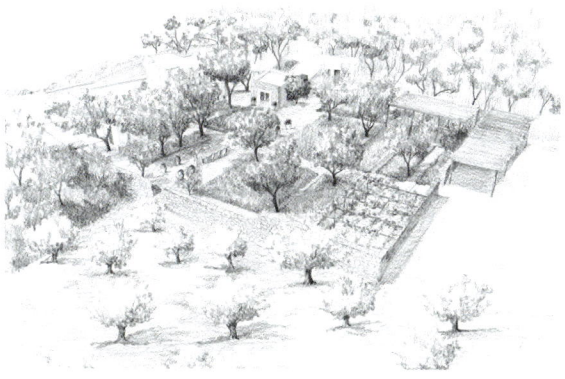

KENSINGTON PALACE GARDENS
London, UK
2011

HOUSE IN KOTTAYAM
With Studio Mumbai
Kerala, India
2011 (see pp. 34–45)

LA CRIQUE
Geneva, Switzerland
2011

HOUSE ON LAKE OWEN
With Pearson Design Group
Wisconsin, USA
2011

LANSDOWNE HOUSE ROOF TERRACE
London, UK
2011

MADRESFIELD COURT
Worcestershire, UK
2011 (see pp. 152–61)

ROLFS FARM: SEED GARDEN
East Sussex, UK
2011

VERGELEGEN
With Olson Kundig
Massachusetts, USA
2011 (see pp. 100–10)

WADHURST PARK
With Ptolemy Dean
Sussex, UK
2011

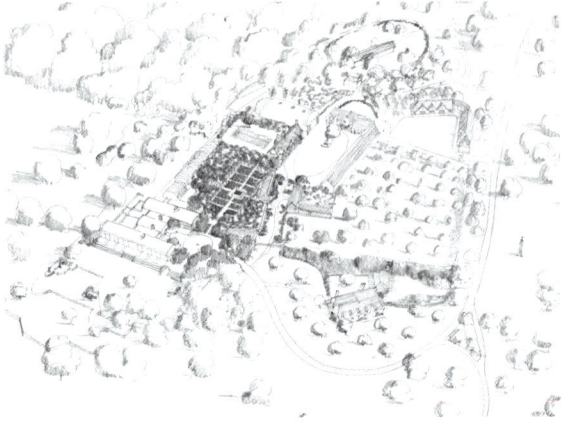

WEST HOUSE
London, UK
2011

ALIBAUG PROJECT
With Studio Mumbai
Maharashtra, India
2012

DUNTISBOURNE HOUSE
With Michaelis Boyd
Gloucestershire, UK
2012

LA GRANJA ALNARDO
With Henning Larsen
Castile and León, Spain
2012 (see pp. 292–301)

HANDSMOOTH HOUSE
With Richard Meier
Oxfordshire, UK
2012

HOWE FARM
Oxfordshire, UK
2012

HOUSE IN ÎLE DE RÉ
Charente-Maritime, France
2012

KEEPERS COTTAGE
Oxfordshire, UK
2012

MAYNES FARM POOL
Hertfordshire, UK
2012

HOUSE IN OAKHILL AVENUE
London, UK
2012

OBSIDIAN
With Alain Bouvier Architects
Mustique, Saint Vincent and the Grenadines
2012

HOUSE IN PELHAM CRESCENT
London, UK
2012

WORMSLEY: PLANTING AROUND HOUSE
Buckinghamshire, UK
2012

HOUSE IN YORK TERRACE
With Make
London, UK
2012

2–6 CANNON STREET POCKET PARK
London, UK
2013–2020

GLEBE VILLAS
With Gumuchdjian Architects
London, UK
2013–2020

A GARDEN IN THE SURREY HILLS
With Axel Vervoordt
Surrey, UK
2013   (see pp. 250–61)

KENNELS LODGE, GOODWOOD
With Ptolemy Dean
Sussex, UK
2013

LE JARDIN SECRET
Marrakech, Morocco
2013   (see pp. 222–31)

NORTHBROOK HOUSE
With John Pardey Architects
Surrey, UK
2013

ROYAL ACADEMY OF ARTS, KEEPER'S GARDEN
London, UK
2013

THE GLEBE
London, UK
2013

TUSMORE PARK
With Johnston Cave
Oxfordshire, UK
2013

HOUSE IN UPPER PHILLIMORE GARDENS
With Formation Architects and Eric Egan
London, UK
2013

CHAPEL FARM
With Smallwood Architects
Rutland, UK
2014

DRONNINGMØLLE BEACH HOUSE
Gribskov, Denmark
2014

FRITHWOOD FARM
Sussex, UK
2014

GORDON HOUSE
With Rose Uniacke
Richmond, Surrey, UK
2014

GÄRTEN DER WELT IGA 2017
Berlin, Germany
2017

RECTORY PARK
With Ptolemy Dean
Kent, UK
2014

ALDOURIE CASTLE
With Ptolemy Dean
Inverness-shire, UK
2015

CORROUR LODGE, COURTYARDS
With Ptolemy Dean
Inverness-shire, UK
2015

HOUSE IN HOLLAND PARK
With Rose Uniacke
London, UK
2015

MIDDLETON LODGE
Yorkshire, UK
2015

CHATSWORTH ROCKERY AND ARCADIA
Derbyshire, UK
2016

CONSTANTINSBORG
Aarhus, Denmark
2016

HOUSE ON YORK TERRACE
London, UK
2016

THE HEPWORTH WAKEFIELD GARDEN
Yorkshire, UK
2016

RHS BRIDGEWATER
With Stephen Hodder Architects
Lancashire, UK
2016

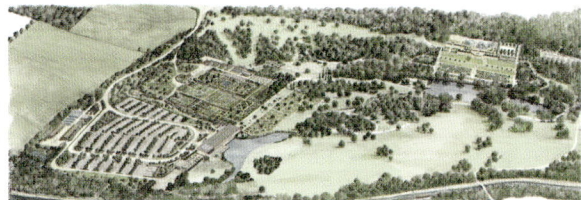

HOUSE IN KENSINGTON
With SheltonMindel
London, UK
2016

VERDE, VICTORIA ROOF GARDEN
With Michael Smith Inc.
London, UK
2016

BATTERSEA PENTHOUSE
With Axel Vervoordt
London, UK
2017

HOPE HOUSE
Sussex, UK
2017

SELFRIDGES ROOF TERRACE
With Alex Cochrane Architects
London, UK
2017

CHELSEA FLOWER SHOW 2018
London, UK
2018

CHELSEA FLOWER SHOW 2019
London, UK
2019

HORTICULTURAL EXPO 2019.
With James Hitchmough
Beijing, China
2019

HORATIO'S GARDEN LONDON
With Stephen Marshall Associates
Stanmore, UK
2019

CHÂTEAU PHÉLAN SÉGUR
Saint-Èstephe, France
2019

MORTON HOUSE, CHISWICK
London, UK
2019

ACKNOWLEDGMENTS

Tim Richardson

I have written a number of books over the years, and therefore several lists of acknowledgments – but I have never felt my thanks more keenly or deeply than in this case.

An extended bout of ill health which commenced in the middle of writing this book meant that my ability to work was considerably impaired. I could not have wished for a more understanding or kinder response from those involved, particularly Tom Stuart-Smith himself, Lucas Dietrich (commissioning editor at T&H) and Sarah Vernon-Hunt as copy editor. Their genuine care and concern for my wellbeing went far beyond anything that might normally be expected in the circumstances. Their solicitude – allowing me to do what I could, when I could – meant that I was spared an extremely stressful and difficult additional burden. I would like to express my sincere thanks to Tom, Lucas and Sarah.

I would like to extend these thanks to the other staff members both in Tom's office and at T&H who had less direct contact with me but were equally kind and careful: Rowan Case, Joanna Lowe and Heather Power at Tom's office, and at Thames & Hudson: Fleur Jones (project editor), Linda Lundin (designer) and Rachel Heley (production). Of course my thanks also goes to them all for doing such a superb job on the production of the book.

During the period of research I made many visits to gardens designed by Tom and I would like to thank the owners, both for giving me access and also in many cases for their personal interactions in the form of interviews and guided tours. It would be slightly invidious to name just a few examples, so suffice to say I am very grateful for this help and in some cases hospitality, as also to the personal assistants and other staff members who facilitated my visits. In every case the head gardeners have been extremely helpful, and I list here those whom I met personally during my research. My thanks goes to them all. Broughton Grange: Andrew Woodhall; Charleville: Owen Mahew; Cogshall Grange: Adrian Lovatt; Culham Court: Simon Rice; Encombe: Simon Hansford; Fort Belvedere: Dean Peckett; A Garden in the Surrey Hills: Greg Amos; Hatch House: Carl Garcia; Oakhill: Joseph Ransley; RHS Wisley: Matt Pottage; Trentham: Michael Walker; Whitehall Farm: Jan Karlik; Windsor Castle: Philip Carter; Yotes Court: Erika Packard.

Finally, redoubled thanks to Tom Stuart-Smith for being so unstintingly helpful, good-humoured and available during the period of the book's production. A number of interviews were conducted at The Barn in Hertfordshire, the home of Tom and Sue Stuart-Smith, and I would like to thank them both for their warm hospitality. This book has been a pleasure and a privilege to write.

Tom Stuart-Smith

My deepest debt of gratitude is to those closest to me. To Sue, my wife and author of *The Well Gardened Mind*, one of the most inspirational and perceptive books ever written about the *why* of gardening. To her, my parents, my five siblings and my children, Rose, Ben and Harry. You created the world in which I have lived, loved and found inspiration.

It is impossible in this space to thank personally the great numbers of people who have collaborated in making these gardens, so I can here only pick out those who have been central to the work shown in this volume. We decided not to mention individual clients in the text, which was a difficult decision, especially as some have been such supportive patrons over many years. Pierre and Catherine Lagrange, Hilary and Galen Weston, Chris and Jill Blundell and Peter Sisseck have all been up for the long haul. Some fellow designers have been especially important to me, because they find landscape critical to the way we experience place and have wanted to engage in the debate. Jamie Fobert, Ptolemy Dean, Bijoy Jain, Andrew Ewing, Axel and Boris Vervoordt and Rose Uniacke have all shaped the way I have worked on shared projects and made them more interesting and nuanced as a result. Then there are the nurseries, the contractors and the gardeners who make it all happen. I have done a lot of work with Crocus, both as a nursery and a contractor, and have always relied on their immense professionalism, led by the brilliant duo of Mark Fane and Peter Clay. Another nursery that was particularly important was Toby and Chris Marchant's Orchard Dene, sadly no more. There are also some wonderful head gardeners whom I have been lucky enough to work with over an extended period of time. Alistair Robertson at various gardens, Andrew Woodhall at Broughton Grange and Michael Walker at Trentham deserve special mention. At home Brian Maslin and Jake Golchin look after the ever-expanding garden with skill, good humour and great patience at the ever-increasing demands I casually throw at them.

Then there are those who are in the same trade and are generous enough to share their expertise and have been in one way or other a source of inspiration. All of them I have known or worked with for at least twenty years, with the exception of James Hitchmough, self-proclaimed eco-botanical maverick, whom I first collaborated with only in 2005. I owe a debt to Penny Hobhouse for pointing me in the right direction, Tania Compton for kick-starting my career, Piet Oudolf for being such a great creative inspiration and for writing so generous a foreword; to Todd Longstaffe-Gowan for being brilliant, outrageous and funny and for sharing an office with me for over twenty years and for introducing me to Jinny Blom.

Then of course there are my wonderful colleagues at Tom Stuart-Smith Ltd, which began with just myself and Kurosh Davis in 1998. Kurosh (amazingly) is still with me as a Director, still playing the viola to concert standards, painting and playing tennis virtually every day. In the early years Andy Hamilton and Jem Hanbury were pivotal to the practice. Now there are four associates: Ed Shackleton, Nick Pusterla, Shankar Kothapuram and Emily Assheton. Jaiji (Frank) Wu has been the bedrock of our technical efforts for the last eight years. Joanna Lowe and latterly Rowan Case in the studio managed our input for this book expertly, and Ruth van Loen kept the whole show on the road. Thank you to all of you and to all those not specifically mentioned here. I know it's not really for me to say, but I think the studio has been both a creative and a happy place.

This book would not be much without the photography. Andrew Lawson and Jerry Harpur were my endlessly generous and creative collaborators in the old days, more recently Marianne Majerus and Andrea Jones have taken most of the beautiful pictures here.

I am very grateful to Lucas Dietrich, Sarah Vernon-Hunt, Fleur Jones, Rachel Heley and Linda Lundin, and Thames & Hudson for their endless patience and professionalism and for producing such a beautiful book.

Finally, huge thanks to Tim for taking this on and for whom the final stages turned out to be rather an epic struggle. Tim contracted Covid 19 early in 2020 and was then seriously affected by the dreaded 'Long Covid'. Through six months of extreme fatigue he somehow managed to keep the same insightful, deeply intelligent eye on the task in hand. It has been a very happy collaboration.

IMAGE CREDITS

All drawings: Tom Stuart-Smith

l = left; r = right; a = above; b = below

Jonathan Buckley 21.
GAP Photos/Marcus Harpur 214, 219, 220, 262–63, 264, 266, 267, 268–69, 270, 271.
Francis Hamel 245.
Ye Hang 317r.
Hufton + Crow 298–99.
Andrea Jones 11, 50–51, 65, 66–67, 68, 70, 71, 72–73, 74, 75, 76–77, 78, 80–81, 82, 83, 84–85, 86, 87, 100–1, 102, 104, 105, 106–7, 108, 109, 129, 140–41, 142, 144–45, 146, 148–49, 150, 151, 156, 160, 250–51, 252, 254–55, 256, 257, 258–59, 260, 261, 291, 292–93, 294, 296, 297, 300, 301, 312bl, 315bl.
James Kerr 16–17, 22–23, 24.
Andrew Lawson 6, 8, 15, 18, 20, 25, 46–47, 48, 52, 54–55, 147, 193, 232–33, 234, 236, 237, 238–39, 240, 304l, 304ar, 304br, 305al, 305r, 306al, 308bl, 308r, 310br.
Marianne Majerus 2, 10, 53, 56, 88–89, 90, 92–93, 94, 95, 96–97, 98, 99, 110–11, 112, 114–15, 116, 117, 118–19, 120, 130–31, 132, 134–35, 136, 137, 138, 139, 152–53, 154, 157, 158–59, 161, 174–75, 176, 178–79, 180, 181, 182–83, 184, 212–13, 218, 221, 222–23, 224, 226, 227, 228–29, 230, 231, 282–83, 284, 286–87, 288, 289, 310l, 312al, 313bl, 313br, 315al, 316ar.
MARKA/Alamy Stock Photo 242.
Derry Moore 34–35, 36, 38–39, 40, 41, 42–43, 44, 45.
Allan Pollok-Morris 26–27, 28, 30–31, 32, 33, 162–63, 164, 166–67, 168, 169, 170–71, 172, 173, 194–95, 196, 199, 204–5, 206, 207, 208, 209, 210, 211, 216–17, 249, 272–73, 274, 276, 277, 278–79, 280, 281, 306bl.
Sabina Rüber 309ar.
Lianne Ryan 316bl.
Cassian Schmidt 127.
Jane Sebire 198, 200–1, 306r.
TSS Ltd 125, 128, 246, 248, 310ar, 314br, 315r, 317bl.
TSS Ltd – Emily Assheton 13, 317al.
TSS Ltd – Luca Puri 307bl.
TSS Ltd – Ed Shackleton 311bl, 313ar, 314ar.
TSS Ltd – Jiaji Wu 124, 314l.
Joe Wainwright 202.

INDEX

Italics indicate illustrations

Barn, The 9, 10, *15*, 46–56, 57–58, 64, 123, *125*, 127–28, *128*, 243
Broughton Grange *7*, *8*, *9*, 16–25, 61, 187, *187*, 189, 190, 192
Charleville 66–75
Cogshall Grange *10*, 91, 110–20, 190
Culham Court *61*, 88–99, 126, 190
Encombe 76–87, 190–91, *190*
Fort Belvedere 69, 174–84
Garden in the Surrey Hills, A 60, 250–61
Granja Alnardo, La *9*, 63, 292–301
Hatch House 282–89
Jardin Secret, La 63, 191, *191*, 222–31
Kottayam, House in 34–45, 63, 188
Madresfield Court 152–61, 186, *186*
Moor Hatches 272–81
Mount St John 126, 187, 190, 219, 232–40
Oakhill 177, 204–11
Snowdenham House 26–33
Trentham *7*, 188, *188*, 194–203, 219
Vergelegen *9*, *11*, 64, 100–10, 301
Whitehall Farm 248, *248*, 262–71
Windsor Castle *10*, 130–39
Wisley, RHS 212–21
Wycliffe Hall 140–51
Yotes Court 162–73

Plants:

Achillea: 'Coronation Gold' 20; *nobilis* 296, *301*
achilleas 52, 126, 146, *220*, 301
Allium: *cristophii* 33, *72–73*; *sphaerocephalon* 21, *33*, *277*
alliums 33, 116, 155, 168, *169*, 203, 235, 240
Ammi: 126; *majus* 58, 256
Amsonia: *hubrichtii* 29, 168, 220; *tabernaemontana* var. *salicifolia* *94*, 168, 289
amsonias 56, 60, 109, 113, 126, 146, 168
Anemanthele lessoniana 52, 276
Anemone x *hybrida* 'Königin Charlotte' 116, *286–87*
Asphodeline liburnica *92–93*, 94, *158–59*
asters 56, 109, 113, 128
Astrantia: *major* 'Claret' 75, 146, 168, 289; 'Roma' 75
astrantias 29, 52, 60, 70, 94, 109, 113, *144–45*, 211, 235

Baptisia australis 168
Bupleurum fruticosum *90*, 256

Calamagrostis: 56; x *acutiflora* 'Karl Foerster' 20, *117*, 120, *288*, 289; *brachytricha* 173
Campanula lactiflora *134–35*; 'Prichard's Variety' 173
campanulas 70, 98, 136, 139, 256
cardoon *18*, 52, 60, 70, 139, *250–51*
carex 113, 266
Carex: *pensylvanica* *106–7*; *testacea* 220, *238–39*, 276

Cenolophium denudatum 59, *164*, *172*
Cephalaria: *dipsacoides* 52; *gigantea* 58, 60
Cercis canadensis 208, 256
cistus 62, *158–59*, 220, 226, 301
Cistus albidus 296, 301
clematis 94, 116, 120, 136, 289
Clematis: 'Étoile Violette' 33; 'Little Nell' 33, 256; 'Madame Julia Correvon' 33; *alpina* 'Willy' 256; *alpina* 'Frances Rivis' 256; *armandii* 'Apple Blossom' 208; *macropetala* 'Lagoon' 256; *viticella* 173
coreopsis 52, 128, 236
cornus 94, 120, 207
Cornus: *alba* 'Sibirica' 208; *controversa* 208; *kousa* 94, *134,–35*, 136, 180, 215, 256
cotinus *92–93*, 94, 120

dahlias 52, 70, 125, 203
darmera 71, 177, 211, 261
delphiniums 70, 236
Deschampsia cespitosa 124, 125
Dianthus carthusianorum 52, *84–85*, 128, 168, 211, *254–55*

Echinacea: *pallida* 60, 126, *204–5*; *paradoxa* 234, *204–5*; *purpurea* 'Magnus' *32*, *116*, *214*, 289; *purpurea* 'Magnus Superior' 113; *purpurea* 'White Swan' *272–73*; *tennesseensis* 'Rocky Top' 236
echinaceas 52, 56, *108*, *112*, 120, 126, 127, 173, 203, 211, *216–17*, *219*, 235, 240
Epimedium rubrum 94, 116, 211
epimediums 75, 173, 184, 208, 220, 256
eremurus 53, *84–85*, 86, 146, 203, *232–33*, 236, 261
Eremurus: 'Joanna' 56, *80–81*; *robustus* 120; *stenophyllus* 220
eryngiums 33, 52, 62, 120, 128, 155, 240
Eryngium: *bourgatii* 289; *giganteum* 59, 113; *yuccifolium* 266; x *zabelii* *21*
Eupatorium maculatum 59; 'Purple Bush' 33, *214*, 215; 'Riesenschirm' *117*; *purpureum* 203, *206*; *rugosum* 'Chocolate' 146
eupatoriums 56, 83, 236, 261, 266, 281
Euphorbia: *characias* subsp. *wulfenii* 208, *288*, 296, 301; *cornigera* *166–67*, 215, *234*; *corollata* 128; *dendroides* 226; *griffithii* 'Dixter' 266; *ingens* 226; *margalidiana* 52; *martini* 289; *mellifera* 173; *nicaeensis* *18*; *oblongata* 256; *palustris* 28, 146, *182–83*; x *pasteurii* 83, 156, *156*; *seguieriana* 236; *tirucalli* 226; *wallichii* 112, 256; 'Whistleberry Garnet' 168, 211
euphorbias 56, 62, 136, *137*, 203, 220, 261, 275, *276*, *280*

foxgloves 52, 59, 120, 126, 136

Gaura lindheimeri 60, 86, 256
Geranium: 'Brookside' 95, *132*, *137*, 139; 'Mayflower' 120; 'Patricia' 20, 29, *54–55*, *157*; *psilostemon* *72–73*; 'Rozanne' 75; *sanguineum* 296, 301
geraniums 56, 86, 94, 109, 156, 173, 208, 235, 276
Gillenia trifoliata 60, 94, *95*, 168, 211

hakonechloa 29, 52, *66–67*, 86, 75, 94, *169*, 208, *210*, *267*, 271, *282–83*, *284*, 289
Helenium: 'Moerheim Beauty' *46–47*, 113, *166–67*, 173, 215, 276, *280*; 'Rubinzwerg' 70
hellebores *30–1*, 116, 122, 208, 220
Hosta: 'Devon Green' *114–15*, 116; *sieboldiana* var. *elegans* 220; *ventricosa* 220
Hydrangea: *arborescens* 'Annabelle' 173, *258–59*, 261; *aspera* 'Villosa group' 33; *heteromalla* 168; *kawakamii* 256; *paniculata* 211; *paniculata* 'Tardiva' 168; *paniculata* 'Kyushu' 139; *petiolaris* 256; *quercifolia* 33, 116, 156, *157*, 208, 256; *serratifolia* 168
Hylotelephium 'Matrona' 52, *219*; 'Munstead Dark Red' *200–1*; *telephium* 'Purple Emperor' *30–31*

Inula magnifica 56; 'Sonnenstrahl' 59
irises 33, 52, 203, 173, 220, 261, 281, 289
Iris: *pseudacorus* 252; *sibirica* 83, *94*, 126; *sibirica* 'Papillon' *182–83*, 211; *sibirica* 'Shirley Pope' *182–83*; *sibirica* 'Silver Edge' 94, *144–45*

lavender 98, 75, 155, 231, *231*, 256
Lilium: 'Citronella' 60; *regale* 236
Liriodendron tulipifera *130–31*, 136, 168, 180, 281

Magnolia: *grandiflora* 136, 173; x *loebneri* 'Leonard Messel' 136; x *loebneri* 'Merrill' 94
magnolias 122, 208, 256
Malus 126, 189; 'Donald Wyman' 289; 'Evereste' 94, 261, 275, 289
Melianthus major 83, 138, 220, 226
miscanthus 20, *22–23*, *24*, 59, 203, 221, 235, *250–51*, 266, 271
Miscanthus sinensis: 'Cascade' 276; 'Ferner Osten' 168, 215, *262–63*; 'Gracillimus' *194–95*; 'Graziella' 276; 'Kleine Silberspinne' 219; 'Malepartus' 56, 60, 70, 146, *170–71*, 236; 'Roland' 211; 'Starlight' *218*
molinia 86, *114–15*, 173, 261, 266
Molinia caerulea: subsp. *arundinacea* 'Transparent' *32*, 156, 168, *218*; subsp. *caerulea* 'Poul Petersen' 116, *118–19*, 208
Monarda 70; *bradburiana* 126; 'Scorpion' 240

Narcissus: 'Actaea' *260*; 'Thalia' 86
nepeta 29, 75, 86, 98, *137*, 155, 236

Nepeta racemosa 'Walker's Low' 276

olive 98, 184, *222–23*, *230*, 231
osmanthus 136, 261

Paeonia: *delavayi* 86; *lactiflora* 'Nymphe' 83
panicum 52, *88–89*, 156, 220
Panicum virgatum: 'Hänse Herms' *219*, 276; 'Shenandoah' 94, 120, 289
Parrotia persica *26–27*, 29, 33, *33*
Pennisetum alopecuroides: 'Cassian's Choice' *250–51*, 256; 'Hameln' 276; 'Moudry' 220
Penstemon: *digitalis* 126; 'Raven' 173
penstemons 52, 125, 126, 128, 211
peonies 70, 94, 98, 126, 136, 173, 151, 184, 236, 261, 275
perovskia 29, *33*, 94, 156, 161, 168, 296
Perovskia 'Blue Spire' 146, *274*
persicaria 20, 83, *166–67*, 236, 261
Persicaria: *amplexicaulis* 4; *amplexicaulis* 'Blackfield' 276; *amplexicaulis* 'Rosea' 139; *amplexicaulis* 'Taurus' *234*
philadelphus 86, 136, 161, 173, 208
phlomis 62, 161, 136, 203, 208, *232–33*, 298, 301
Phlomis: *italica* 276; *russeliana* 20, 60, *211*, 220, 236
phlox 20, *28*, 29, *33*, 59, 63, 94, 109, 146, 156, 173
Phlox: *paniculata*: 'Blue Paradise' 173; *paniculata* 'Eventide' 173; *paniculata* 'Franz Schubert' 173, 219, *272–73*; *pilosa* 211
pulmonaria 173, 220
Pulmonaria 'Blue Ensign' 94

rodgersia 63, 281
Rodgersia: *pinnata* 'Superba' *74*, 219; *podophylla* 116
Rosa: *banksiae* var. *normalis* 161; *glauca* *72–73*; *nutkana* 'Plena' *87*; x *odorata* 'Mutabilis' 98, 116, 161, 256, 275, *276*; *rugosa* 'Roseraie de l'Hay' *138*; *rugosa* 'Schneezwerg' *258–59*; *sanguinea* 256; *soulieana* 125
Rose 'Aimée Vibert' 83; 'Albertine' 289; 'Blanc Double de Coubert' 139; 'Blush Noisette' 289; 'Buff Beauty' 256; 'Cécile Brunner' 86; 'Cornelia' 156, 177; 'Étoile de Hollande' 275, 289; 'Francis E. Lester' 83, 289; 'Ghislaine de Féligonde' 161; 'Gruss an Aachen' 155; 'Guinée' 275; 'Kew Gardens' *158–59*, 161; 'Madame Alfred Carrière' 86; 'Malvern Hills' 161, 289; 'Moonlight' 156, 261; 'Munstead Wood' 155; 'Nyveldt's White' 136; 'Rambling Rector' 136; 'Seagull' 136; 'Souvenir du Docteur Jamain' 161; 'Veilchenblau' 156; 'Wild Edric' 155
roses 56, *68*, 70, 75, *78*, *84–85*, 94,

124, 136, 155, 156, *161*, 173, 177, 184, 275, 289
Rudbeckia: *fulgida* var. *deamii* 56; *maxima* 70, *116*, 236; *missouriensis* 211
rudbeckias 113, 116, 128, 203, 220, 240

Salvia: 'Amistad' 139; *canariensis* 226; *chamaedryoides* 226; *nemorosa* 'Amethyst' 29, *160*, *166–67*, 168, 219; *nemorosa* 'Ostfriesland' 52; *officinalis* 301; *pomifera* 226; *sclarea* var. *turkestanica* 301; x *sylvestris* 'Blauhugel' 20, 240; x *sylvestris* 'Mainacht' 240
salvias 56, 62, 86, 94, 109, 113, 126, 156, 161, 203, 219, *234*, 236, 276, *277*, 296
sanguisorba 83, 235, 266
Sanguisorba: *canadensis* 219; *officinalis* 'Red Thunder' *206*, 275; *officinalis* 'Tanna' 33
santolina 256, *296*, 300
Santolina: *chamaecyparissus* 296; *rosmarinifolia* 296, 301
sedums 29, 33, 56, 126, *198*, 203, 220, 235, *238–39*, 240, 275, *278–79*
Selinum wallichianum 71, *114–15*, 120, 116
Silphium: *laciniatum* 128, *206*, 211; *terebinthinaceum* 206
Sporobolus heterolepis 104, 126, 276
stipa *33*, 98, 113, 126, 156, 161, 230, 276
Stipa: *barbata* 301; *brachytricha* 94, 120, *calamagrostis* *28*, 29, *54–55*, *214*, 220, 236; *gigantea* 58, 59, *158–59*, *200–1*, *294*; *extremiorientalis* 220; *tenuissima* *84–85*, *227*, 231, *277*

thalictrum 59, 60, 220, 235, 276
Thalictrum: *aquilegifolium* *144–45*; *delavayi* 33, 52; *rochebruneanum* 203
tulips *16–17*, 24, 33, *56*, 113, 276; 'Abu Hassan' 33; 'Ballerina' 33; 'Havran' 33; 'Helmar' 33; 'Queen of Night' 139

verbascum *48*, 56, 125, 139, 155, 161, 203, 220, 256, 261
Verbascum: *bombyciferum* 'Arctic Summer' 60, *254–55*; *lychnitis* 235; *olympicum* *22–23*
Verbena: *bonariensis* 58, *209*, 256, *282–83*, *284*; *hastata* f. *rosea* 281
Veronicastrum virginicum 33; 'Apollo' 168; 'Fascination' 60, 146, 215, 289; 'Lavendelturm' *164*, 173, 203; 'Spring Dew' 211, 281; 'Temptation' 281
veronicastrums 20, *48*, 52, 56, 59, 63, 94, *208*, *209*, 235, 240, 266, *282–83*

yew, Irish 20, *21*, *25*, *48*, 146, *148–49*, *196*, 197, 203

zelkova 207, 208